GREAT LIVES OBSE

Gerald Emanuel Ste

EACH VOLUME IN THE SERIES VIEWS THE CHARACTERS AND ACHIEVE-
MENT OF A GREAT WORLD FIGURE IN THREE PERSPECTIVES—
THROUGH HIS OWN WORDS, THROUGH THE OPINIONS OF HIS CON-
TEMPORARIES, AND THROUGH RETROSPECTIVE JUDGMENTS—THUS
COMBINING THE INTIMACY OF AUTOBIOGRAPHY, THE IMMEDIACY
OF EYEWITNESS OBSERVATION, AND THE OBJECTIVITY OF MODERN
SCHOLARSHIP.

BENJAMIN QUARLES, *the editor of this volume in the Great
Lives Observed series, is Professor of History at Morgan State
College. A noted scholar and a Guggenheim Fellow, Quarles
is the author of many books, including* Frederick Douglass,
Lincoln and the Negro, *and* The Negro in the Making of
America. *His numerous articles, monographs, and book reviews
appear frequently in scholarly and popular publications.*

Forthcoming volumes in the Great Lives Observed series

John Calhoun, *edited by Margaret L. Coit*

Hitler, *edited by George H. Stein*

Lloyd George, *edited by Martin Gilbert*

Huey Long, *edited by Hugh Graham*

Mao, *edited by Jerome Ch'en*

Booker T. Washington, *edited by Emma Lou Thornbrough*

Woodrow Wilson, *edited by John Braeman*

GREAT LIVES OBSERVED

Frederick
Douglass

Edited by BENJAMIN QUARLES

A SPECTRUM BOOK

PRENTICE-HALL, INC., ENGLEWOOD CLIFFS, N.J.

To my daughter, Pam

Contents

v

vi

vii

Introduction

When Frederick Douglass was born, the day was unnoted, and it was not even certain that the year was 1817. For he was born a slave on a plantation in Maryland. But when he died, five state legislatures adopted resolutions of regret, and a Washington *Post* editorial stated that he "died in an epoch which he did more than any other to create." At his last rites, held in Washington on a winter afternoon in 1895, two Senators and a Supreme Court justice were numbered among the honorary pall bearers, and on that funeral day the colored schools of the District were closed in his honor.

Despite his humble birth, the man they mourned had been in the limelight for nearly half a century. During his span he had won a wide reputation as an abolitionist lecturer possessed of a fluent tongue, a newspaper editor, a recruiter for Union troops in the Civil War, a spokesman for the newly freed slaves, and the holder of three federal appointments beginning in 1877, when President Hayes named him as United States Marshal for the District of Columbia. In any careful study of the abolitionist crusade and related reforms, and of the significant role of the Negro in the Civil War and Reconstruction periods, one is bound to meet Douglass at every turn.

In the beginning stages of his career as a reformer, Douglass undoubtedly owed much to the fact that he had been a slave. Hence he could speak and write from a firsthand knowledge of life as an underling on a plantation. Moreover he himself furnished an indictment of slavery with his ease of expression, his obvious intelligence, and his responsible behavior in all his dealings, private and public. Possibly some of those who listened to a Douglass lecture came away with doubts whether the speaker had actually been a slave.

No impostor, Douglass was born on the Eastern Shore of Maryland, in Talbot County, the slave of Captain Aaron Anthony. When he was seven, his mother died; she had been hired out and he had only seen her four or five times in his life. Shortly thereafter Douglass was sent to Baltimore to work for Hugh Auld, a distant relative of Captain Anthony. For seven years, relatively pleasant ones for the young slave, he worked as a houseboy and then as a laborer in Auld's shipyard. During this span Douglass succeeded in learning to read and write. Initially he was helped by his mistress, but her husband soon objected, pointing out that "learning" would spoil the best slave in the world. Not to be deterred, Douglass turned to seeking instruction from young white boys, offering them food in exchange for an impromptu reading lesson from *The Columbian Orator,* a book of popular declamation for which he had paid fifty cents.

To "those little Baltimore boys," as he later referred to them, Douglass developed a feeling of attachment. But this link was broken in March, 1832, when the death of Captain Anthony placed him in possession of Anthony's son-in-law, Thomas Auld, who lived at St. Michaels, 40 miles below Baltimore.

The return to the Eastern Shore did not prove to Douglass's advantage. "My master and myself had a number of differences," he wrote. To Douglass, Auld was mean—badly underfeeding his slaves —and inordinately fond of the whip. After nine months of strained relations between master and slave, Douglass was hired out to Edward Covey, whose reputation as a slave-breaker enabled him to get young slaves to till his farm at little or no expense.

During the first six months of his stay with Covey, Douglass's back was generally sore from cowskin blows. But one hot day in August, 1833, the tables were turned, and "a slave was made a man," as Douglass put it. When Covey attempted to apply the whip, Douglass fought back, and for many minutes the two exchanged blows and wrestled. At length Covey, puffing and beginning to lose blood, called a halt. He never again attempted to lay a hand on Douglass.

Five months later Douglass was placed in the employ of William Freeland, who gave his slaves enough to eat and who permitted Douglass to teach them to read on Sundays and evenings. According to Douglass, Freeland was the best master he ever had "until I became my own master." But this was the rub, for Douglass had resolved to become free, vowing on January 1, 1836, that he would make the attempt before the year was out.

To this end he conceived a plan to paddle down the Chesapeake from the Freeland farm—three miles from St. Michaels—to the head of the bay, 70 miles away, and then to strike out on foot. Douglass made careful plans, including the preparing of passes for his companions. But on the morning of the get-away day the five conspirators were suddenly rounded up, their plans having been divulged, possibly by a slave who had previously changed his mind about making the break. As leader of the abortive plot, Douglass was put in chains and lodged in jail.

Douglass was in dread lest he be sold to a plantation in the lower South as a punishment. But his master, perhaps troubled in conscience, sent him back to Baltimore with a promise of freedom when he became 25. Put to work again in a ship-yard, Douglass became an expert calker in a year's time, commanding the top wage of one dollar and a half a day. A quarrel with his master over money strengthened Douglass's determination to make another attempt to escape. Moreover he had become engaged to Anna Murray, a free Negro then employed as a housekeeper for a wealthy family. The two had become acquainted while attending meetings of the East Baltimore Improvement Society, one of the 35 benevolent organizations formed by the Negroes of the city.

Possessed of $17, some of it furnished by Anna, and borrowing a "protection"—a paper given to free Negro seamen who came ashore in Southern ports—Douglass boarded a train going northward. Fortunately for him the conductor gave only a perfunctory glance at the "protection" as he collected the fare. At Wilmington, his heart still beating fast, Douglass took the boat for Philadelphia. From there he took a night train to New York, arriving on the morning of September 4, 1838, feeling "like one who had escaped a den of hungry lions," as he put it at the time.

If his heart no longer pounded, the still suspicious Douglass was loath to confide in anyone, black or white. But he had no choice, knowing no one in New York. Years later he would claim that he was "not a bad reader of the human face." At any rate, he picked out a sailor who in turn put him in the best of hands, those of David Ruggles, who as secretary of the New York Vigilance Committee spent much of his time in assisting runaways. Ruggles in truth was, as Douglass described him, "a whole-souled man, fully imbued with a love of his afflicted and hunted people." Ruggles provided a lodging-place for Douglass while he awaited the arrival of Anna to whom he had written. The marriage ceremony was performed gratis by Reverend James W. C. Pennington, like Douglass, a runaway from Maryland. Ruggles advised the newlyweds to go to New Bedford, Massachusetts, where Douglass, as a calker, might find employment.

Once at New Bedford, Douglass was unable to work at his trade, his skin color nullifying his skills. But he took whatever jobs that came his way, sawing wood, digging cellars, shoveling coal, blowing bellows, and stevedoring. An odd-jobs laborer no matter how persevering would find it hard to get ahead. Anna therefore took employment as a domestic until the birth of Rosetta in June, 1839. A year and a half later another child, Lewis, joined the family circle.

Douglass's responsibilities as a husband and a father did not prevent him from taking an interest in church affairs and in the abolitionist crusade. He had intended to join a white Methodist church, but unable to accept segregated arrangements in seating and at the communion table, he left to take membership in the Negro-controlled Zion Methodist church. Broadening his concerns, he began to attend meetings of Negro abolitionists, gradually taking a more important part in the proceedings. In June, 1839, he was in the chair when such a group drew up a resolution condemning the colonization movement to send Negroes to Africa. Negroes had vigorously opposed the colonization since the founding of the American Colonization Society in 1816. Their dissent had been vigorously seconded by William Lloyd Garrison who, after having launched his weekly, *The Liberator*, in January, 1831, had won an unmatched reputation as a foe to slavery.

Douglass had become a reader of *The Liberator*, and he shared the hero-worshipping admiration which most Negroes felt for its editor. In August, 1841, Douglass met Garrison at abolitionist meetings in New Bedford and Nantucket. The latter marked a turning point in the career of the former slave. Called upon to speak with no advance warning, Douglass managed to say something that held the attention of his 500 listeners. It was the only speech he ever gave of which he could not recall a single line afterward. But it must have been effective. At any rate, Garrison arose as if on cue, and gave one of the most stirring addresses of his entire career, using Douglass's remarks as a text. When the meeting was over, the general agent of the Massachusetts Anti-Slavery Society asked Douglass to become an agent of the Society. Douglass accepted, stipulating that he would try it for three months, thinking that by then his usefulness to the abolitionists would have ended. But he had found his calling, and would never again roll casks on the wharf or make use of his calking tools.

Douglass spent the next four years under the wing of the Massachusetts abolitionists. This band of earnest men and women, led by Garrison and Wendell Phillips, prince of orators, lived at a time when reform movements flourished. Garrison and his followers bore the banners of many of these programs for human betterment, but their greatest zeal went into the abolitionist crusade. They considered slavery the greatest evil under the sun, opposing it, they alleged, for what it did to the slave, for what it did to the master, and for what it did to such civil liberties as freedom of speech, freedom of the press, and trial by jury.

To bear witness against slavery the Garrisonians were naturally pleased to recruit a fugitive from the system. Their gratification with Douglass deepened with every passing month. People came to see Douglass as well as to listen to him. In truth he was an imposing figure. Six feet tall, broad-shouldered, his hair worn long, as was the custom, and neatly parted on the side, his eyes deep-set and steady, nose well-formed, lips full and skin bronze-colored, he looked like someone destined for the platform or pulpit. A face not likely to be forgotten was not his only asset. His voice struck the ear pleasantly, and as he gained experience, he capitalized on it to the full. Melodious and strong, it varied in speed and pitch according to its use to convey wit, sarcasm, argument, or invective.

To a speaking voice meant for the rostrum he brought the content of a logical mind. In his first weeks as a traveling agent and lecturer, he devoted himself to a simple narration of his experience before freedom. Then from a description of slavery he began to go into a more direct denunciation of it. Gradually in his public appearances he broadened his subject matter, attacking the church in the North for its timidity on slavery, demanding the abolition of slavery in the District of Columbia, speaking to raise funds on behalf of runaways like himself, and protesting against the annexation of Texas.

Although an agent for the Massachusetts Society, Douglass did not work exclusively in the Bay State. Within three months he was in Rhode Island working to defeat the adoption of a state constitution that barred Negroes from voting. During the following summer he spent several weeks in western New York, and in the summer of 1843 he made a Western tour of three months, much of which was spent in Ohio and Indiana. Not everywhere were abolitionist reformers welcome, particularly dark-skinned ones. Sometimes he and his companions were greeted with catcalls or "a shower of pro-slavery eggs." At Pendleton, Ohio, Douglass was severely beaten, after a vain attempt at self-defense, and left in a state of unconsciousness. He was quickly revived, although he was some time in regaining the full use of his right hand, the broken bones having not been properly set.

During the winter of 1844–45, Douglass curtailed his lecturing activities to give more time to the writing of a book describing his life as a slave. His *Narrative of the Life of Frederick Douglass* appeared in the spring of 1845. Not ghost-written like so many autobiographies by former slaves, the *Narrative* impelled the reader to turn the page. Storytelling in tone, it was absorbing in its sensitive descriptions of places and persons, including a sharply etched portrait of slave-breaker Covey. Designed to hasten "the glad day of deliverance to the millions of my brethren in bonds," as its concluding sentence points out, the *Narrative* was a moving document. Boosted by good press notices and reviews, it became a bestseller on two continents, over 30,000 copies being sold in five years.

A noteworthy addition to the campaign literature of abolitionism, the *Narrative* marked another source of Douglass's growing influence—a facility with the written word. Dating from his early months as a lecturing agent, Douglass had shown an inclination to put his thoughts on paper, and the *Narrative* clearly foreshadowed the influence he would wield through the printed page.

With his book completed, Douglass was ready to take a step that had been lodging in his mind for many months—a trip to the British Isles. Making provision for his family, his children now numbering four, he took passage on a Cunard liner, arriving at Liverpool in late August, 1845. For 21 months he toured England, Ireland, and Scotland, often alone but sometimes in company with other reformers, native-born or American. His sojourn was all he could have wished for. His audiences were large and sympathetic. Equally warming was the treatment he received in hotels and other places of public accommodation.

Douglass made many friends and won many admirers. A group of well-wishers negotiated his freedom legally, raising $700 to send to his former master. Douglass met stage and literary celebrities, and he made the acquaintance of Parliamentary leaders Richard Cobden and John Bright. One of his most treasured experiences was a dinner engagement with the venerable Thomas Clarkson, who had done so much to abolish slavery in the British West Indies.

Douglass's avowed reason for making the trip was to strike at American slavery, and he succeeded in dealing it some hard blows. Without doubt, he influenced British public opinion. His cordial reception and the response he evoked would soon lead other Negro reformers to cross the Atlantic, repeating his message and thereby deepening the mass hostility to slavery that became so evident in England during the Civil War.

Upon his return to the United States, Douglass decided to publish a weekly newspaper. Funds were available, British friends having raised $2,175 for the venture. Garrison voiced his opposition. But Douglass, anxious to test his own abilities to the full, cut his ties with the Massachusetts abolitionists and moved to Rochester, in western New York. On December 3, 1848, the first issue of his weekly, *The North Star*, made its appearance.

Douglass brought out a newspaper for 15 years, despite chronic and pressing money problems. His work as an editor contributed markedly to his mental development, forcing him to study and to think in preparation for writing his editorials and articles. It required him to express himself in clear and forceful prose. Moreover, in financial matters, as in taking a stand on public issues, heading a newspaper forced him to "lean upon himself," as he phrased it. Douglass's journal enabled other Negroes—essayists, columnists, letter-writers, and poets—to find an outlet for their ideas, viewpoints, and literary flights. Even non-contributing Negroes could take pride in a well-edited newspaper, one that compared favorably with the better weeklies of the day. White readers, too, could hardly help receiving favorable impressions that would seem to belie the charge of Negro inferiority. Indeed Douglass appended his initials to his editorials in order to demonstrate that a former slave could write good English.

With a newspaper to supplement his speaking appearances on the public platform, Douglass was doubly armed to become a "terror to evildoers." Although his range of interests tended to expand, he never forgot that the main target was slavery. In addition to speaking and writing about it, he took part in a more direct expression of protest—the Underground Railroad. A former runaway himself, he was strongly in sympathy with those who made the dash for freedom. The fees from many of his lectures went to help fugitives.

When he went to his printing shop in the mornings, it was not unusual for him to find runaways sitting on the steps, waiting for him. He knew where to take them until night fell—to a sail loft, to a barn, or to the quiet home of a trusted sympathizer. When darkness fell, he sped them on their way to the Canadian border. In one period of two weeks in May, 1854, he aided over 30 to reach the Queen's dominions.

From helping the runaway slave to assisting the Negro already free was a natural progression for Douglass. "Improving my free colored Brethren," was the chief reason he gave for launching a newspaper. With such a goal, Douglass inevitably became a major figure in the colored convention movement. Beginning in 1830, Negro leaders had held periodic meetings to make clear their attitude on public issues and to take concerted action thereon. At the meeting held in Cleveland in 1848, Douglass was chosen president. Five years later he was one of the dominant figures at the Rochester Colored National Convention, the most important assembly of the entire movement. As chairman of the Committee on Declaration of Sentiments, he read the committee resolutions whose essence was caught in one of their arresting lines: "We ask that in our native land we shall not be treated as strangers."

Douglass's interest in the welfare of the Negro led him to become an advocate of industrial education. He urged colored youths to learn trades and become skilled laborers. An opponent of Jim Crow wherever it appeared, Douglass constantly courted trouble by ignoring the "White Only" signs in public places. Late in 1848, he wrote a long letter to the editor of the Rochester *Courier* strongly protesting the action of the principal of a local girl's school in putting his nine-year-old daughter in a classroom by herself. Douglass had little patience with Negro barbers whose trade was exclusively white, and he expressed his displeasure with Elizabeth Taylor Greenfield for singing at concert halls where Negroes were barred, informing her that she should drop the sobriquet, "The Black Swan," exchanging it for "The White Raven."

But if Douglass was second to none in his efforts to promote the advancement of the Negro, this is not to say that his concerns were solely racial. To him the struggle of the colored man was a phase of the larger, human struggle. Hence he gave attention to some reforms which were not race-centered. He was opposed to capital punishment, holding that it was "repulsive" to the best interests of humanity. Believing that hard drink was synonymous with poverty and crime, and a teetotaler himself, he was a temperance advocate. In March, 1848, he addressed the Rochester Temperance Society, the first time any predominantly white group had ever invited him to speak on a topic other than the Negro. In 1852, he attended the organizational meeting of the New York Woman's State Temperance Convention, held in Rochester.

However it was the woman's rights movement that enlisted Douglass's keenest interest. In this movement he was truly among the pioneers. In the America in which he came to manhood, women did not stand equal to men in the eyes of the law, being denied the right to make contracts, to testify in courts, and to vote. Douglass took a stand against these restrictions, even though any man who spoke up for woman's rights became a fair target for ridicule and innuendo. The first issue of Douglass's weekly carried on its masthead the line, "Right is of no sex."

Seven months later, at Seneca Falls, New York, the woman's rights movement in America was formally launched. At this historic meeting, Douglass took a prominent part, being the only man to do so. Many of the delegates to the convention were hesitant about asserting that women should have the franchise, but not Douglass. His speech to the effect that political equality was vital to the women's cause led to the adoption of a resolution affirming the right to vote.

Douglass's stand on the suffrage issue was the key to much of his reform emphasis in the 1850's—a belief in the power of the ballot. When he was in Massachusetts, he had been a non-voting abolitionist, following the moral-suasionist approach of the Garrison-Phillips school of reformers. But when he moved to Rochester he found himself among the political abolitionists, and he soon joined them. Now he would pursue his goals by vote as well as by voice and pen.

In 1851, Douglass's newspaper became the official organ of the Liberty party. Born in 1840, this party had experienced a fitful career, now almost over. Its followers had gone over to the Free Soil party, a trend which continued in 1852, despite the efforts of Douglass and his associates. In 1856, the Liberty party diehards formed themselves into the Radical Abolitionist party, Douglass being one of the signers of the call.

But in the presidential election of that year the party could not have polled more than a few hundred votes. In 1858, the party put up a candidate for governor, Gerrit Smith, a long-time patron of Douglass, but Smith was ignored by the voters, despite Douglass's electioneering. By 1859, the Radical Abolitionists were far closer to their goal than they could have discerned, the North and the South having drifted so far apart as to create a war psychosis.

Douglass was a confidant of the man who became the Civil War martyr in the North, John Brown. As early as November, 1848, Douglass visited Brown at Springfield, Massachusetts, at the latter's invitation. The two reformers became friends almost at sight. In February, 1858, nearly ten years later, Brown was a house guest at the Douglass home in Rochester. Here it was that he drafted his blueprint for his native land, a document termed the "Provisional Constitution and Ordinance for the People of the United States." Twenty months later Brown attempted to seize the government arsenal at Harpers Ferry, only to be arrested on October 16, 1859. On hearing the alarming news Douglass fled the country, having been forewarned by a friendly telegraph operator that a warrant had been issued for his arrest as an accomplice of Brown.

Five months later Douglass returned to America, cutting short his second trip to the British Isles upon learning of the death of

Annie, his fifth and last child. Douglass reached Rochester to find that Annie had been buried in the family lot of a white abolitionist who had come to the rescue of Mrs. Douglass after the city authorities refused her the use of the publicly-owned cemetery. If the summer of 1860 marked a low point in Douglass's career, it was of short duration. Lincoln's election in November brought about the secession of the Southern states. Six weeks after he took office, he issued a call for 75,000 volunteers to put down the rebellion.

The coming of the war had a tonic effect on Douglass; to him the conflict was a crusade for freedom, nothing more and certainly nothing less. Because to him the purpose of the war was the emancipation of the slaves, he was anxious that the Negro himself strike a blow. He urged colored men to form militia companies, and in the columns of his journal he advised Lincoln to enlist Negroes, free and slave, into "a liberating army," to march into the Confederacy, freeing its bondmen.

When it quickly became evident that the cautious Lincoln, his ear to the ground, could not be rushed into using the Negro, Douglass's criticisms took on a sharp tone. But, as with other reformers, his strictures grew milder as "the slow coach at Washington" finally began to pick up speed. Lincoln's signing of the Emancipation Proclamation pleased Douglass, especially since it gave the presidential stamp of approval to the recruiting of Negro troops. Douglass described January 1, 1863, as "a day for poetry and song."

Too old to bear arms himself, Douglass served as a recruiting agent, traveling through the North exhorting Negroes to sign up. He was especially proud of enrolling two of his own sons. But he soon found that his job as a recruiter was made more difficult by the pattern of discrimination against the Negro soldier. Succeeding in obtaining an interview with Lincoln, Douglass told him of the grievances of the Negro volunteer—his lower pay per month, his slim chances of being promoted, and his likelihood of receiving peculiarly harsh treatment if captured by the enemy. Lincoln was sympathetic, but he parried Douglass's contentions, pointing out that public opinion must be considered in matters relating to the Negro.

Not wholly discouraged, Douglass believed that the administration was ready to grant a commission to a Negro. Losing no time as he left the White House, he went to the War Office and informed Secretary Stanton that he was available for a military commission. Douglass left the Secretary's office under the impression that his mission had been successful. Hastening to Rochester he brought out the final issue of his journal, informing his readers that he was about to become an assistant adjutant general on the staff of Lorenzo Thomas. The announcement was premature: no commission ever arrived. Disillusioned with military affairs, Douglass returned to the lecture platform.

A year later, in August, 1864, he had a second audience with Lincoln, this time at the latter's request. The two men discussed a plan, broached by Lincoln, for assisting slaves to escape prior to peace negotiations in case the North was compelled to grant peace terms to the Confederacy. Douglass asked permission to give the matter further thought. But there was no need, as it turned out. The North's fortunes took a sharp turn for the better with the fall of Atlanta, and all talk of a negotiated peace was forgotten. Northern success on the battlefield greatly improved Lincoln's chances of re-election.

As the war drew to a close, Douglass was able to concentrate his efforts on the suffrage. With the coming of peace and the passing of slavery, the ballot became more important than ever. For it was a cardinal belief of Douglass that the newly freed Negro must have the vote in order to protect and maintain his liberty. "I set myself to work," wrote Douglass, "with whatever force and energy I possessed to secure this power for the recently-emancipated slaves." Douglass needed all of his resources. White Southerners and their supporters stressed the point that the freedmen were ignorant of public affairs and hence unfit to exercise full citizenship. And even in the North with its relatively sparse Negro population, Negro suffrage ran counter to public opinion, most states forbidding or limiting it.

Negro leaders sought the support of President Andrew Johnson, successor to the revered Lincoln. On February 7, 1866, a delegation of five Negroes called at the White House. Through their two spokesmen, of whom Douglass was one, they expressed the hope that the President would support the movement for Negro suffrage.

Johnson gave them no satisfaction, pointing out in essence that such a step would lead to a race war. Not permitted to refute Johnson's allegations, the delegation withdrew and, caucusing immediately, authorized Douglass to formulate a reply. Douglass completed his statement within a few hours, anxious that it reach the morning newspapers at the same time as the release from the White House.

But Negro suffrage, whatever Johnson's attitude, could not be stayed. The Republican party needed votes in the South, and they were to be found among the former slaves who could be expected to vote for the party of Abraham Lincoln. Hence the Republican-dominated Congress passed measures to make Negro voting and office-holding a reality. As might be expected, Douglass was a staunch supporter of the Republican party, crediting it with having saved the Union, abolished slavery, and made the Negro a soldier and a citizen.

Douglass's party loyalty was rewarded, in 1877, by his appointment as Marshal of the District of Columbia. It must be added, however, that the appointment stemmed in part from President Hayes's desire to placate the Negroes for his withdrawal from the South of the remaining federal troops, the backbone of the Republican-Negro regimes. But Douglass did not care to argue as to the motives of the President, preferring to regard the appointment as a breakthrough, a Negro "first." But Douglass could not avoid trying to explain Hayes's subsequent action in taking from the the Marshal's office the functions of attending presidential receptions and introducing guests at the White House on state occasions.

The functions of the Marshal's office included the surveillance of criminals, and for this aspect of the job Douglass had little liking. But otherwise he found the appointment "in every way agreeable." He selected able subordinates, particularly in the case of the Assistant Marshal. The most conspicuous duty of the Marshal's office was that of escort at a Presidential inauguration, accompanying both the outgoing and incoming Chief Executive. On March 4, 1881, Douglass led the solemn march from the Senate chamber to the Capitol rotunda, where James A. Garfield took the oath of office and then delivered his inaugural address.

The new President had someone else in mind for Marshal, but he rewarded Douglass with appointment as Recorder of Deeds of the District of Columbia. Douglass readily accepted, although Garfield had previously promised to retain him as Marshal. Douglass was somewhat mollified by an invitation to the White House, where Garfield spoke of his intention to appoint Negro diplomats to white nations. Although having reason to feel unsure of Garfield's promises, Douglass believed him to be entirely sincere in the proposal to send Negroes to posts abroad other than Haiti or Liberia. But the assassination of Garfield put an end to speculation as it did to hope.

Even though a government official, Douglass, happily for him, never had to hold his tongue on public issues. During his years as Marshal and Recorder, he continued to inveigh against policies he considered unwise, against practices which he considered unjust and prejudice-ridden. His words carried weight, particularly in Negro circles—almost unsought he had become the figure to whom the mass of Negroes looked for leadership. To be sure there were other Negroes of ability, and with a following of sorts. But they were overshadowed by Douglass. Standing in the wings were Booker T. Washington and W. E. B. DuBois, but neither was ready to step to the center of the stage until 1895, the year Douglass died.

Hence in the seventies and eighties it was to Douglass that the colored rank and file turned for pronunciamentos on matters affecting the race. A protester without peer, Douglass could be depended upon to thunder against things which Negroes regarded as prejudicial and unjust—the ruling of the Supreme Court in the Civil Rights Cases, and suppression of the Negro vote in the South, the leasing out of convicts as laborers, the crop-lien system, and lynch law. On less clearcut issues the colored people looked to Douglass for the correct viewpoint, be it the annexation of Santo Domingo, the exclusion of the Chinese, or the Negro exodus from the South.

Some correspondents looked to Douglass for more than advice and counsel. Reputed to be rich, he received many begging letters. Many of these came from ne'er-do-wells, although not in the case of the gifted Henry O. Tanner, who besought a donation for the purchase of his painting, "Bag-Pipe Lesson," to have it presented to the Hampton Institute Library. The caterer, George T. Downing, wrote that he was "striving for the Senate restaurant," and asked

Douglass to enlist the support of six prominent Republican incumbents. Other Negroes sought recommendations for high posts; on-the-make lesser knowns, like Ida B. Wells, asked him to furnish them with letters of introduction to influential persons.

If Douglass was the most prominent and powerful Negro of his day, it cannot be denied that there was a sizeable corps of detractors within the color line. There was, as one of Douglass's correspondents put it, "a certain set of Negroes in the country who believe the only way to fame or favor (without the possession of brains) is to 'criticize Fred Douglass.'" Some church-going Negroes resented Douglass's criticism of the "emotional, shouting and thoughtless religion," observable in many colored congregations. Douglass's second marriage exposed him to criticism. In January, 1884, two years after Anna's death, Douglass married a dignified white woman of 45, Helen Pitts. He knew such a step would meet with raised eyebrows, but he believed that a person branded himself coward if he refrained from doing the right thing for fear of public opinion.

Predictably many Negroes voiced objection to the marriage, charging Douglass with abandoning the race, among other things. Douglass felt that their criticisms were unsound; he held that he had not deserted the Negro. On the contrary, this crowning act of his private life was a demonstration that the two races could live in amicable equality under the same roof. He deemed his marriage to a white woman as a burning protest against color prejudice and separatism.

For Douglass was not a self-segregator; he might indeed be called a mainstream Negro. He believed that the true mission of America was to remove barriers between its people, making for mobility rather than rigidity. He was too careful a thinker to believe that a Negro organization—church, club, fraternity, lyceum group—was inferior by virtue of its being Negro. Indeed, he attended a Negro church—the African Methodist Episcopal Metropolitan church in Washington (although he never became a member, despite the pastor's cordial invitation). But he did not believe that separation was the solution of the Negro problem.

In 1886, Douglass found himself free for a belated honeymoon. The Republican party had lost the election of 1884, and Douglass eventually but inevitably found himself off the federal payroll. Thus free, he and Helen proceeded to arrange a tour abroad. They left in September, 1886, and for the next 11 months they traveled throughout Western Europe and the Near East. In the main they followed the beaten tourist trail, although they made it a point to visit such spots as the Protestant Cemetery in Florence where they might view the grave of abolitionist Theodore Parker. In the British Isles Douglass renewed friendships dating back 40 years. Nearly three months of the couple's time was spent in Paris. Here they met Victor Schoelcher, who, in 1848, had framed the decree that freed the slaves in the French colonies. The aged member of the French Senate came to have a high regard for Douglass, stipulating, in 1890, that his biography of Toussaint L'Ouverture could be translated into English only if Douglass wrote an introduction for it.

Shortly after his return to Washington, Douglass's Negro admirers gave him a public reception. But Negroes were not the only group that welcomed Douglass home. The Republican party, seeking to regain control of the White House, had work for its leading vote-getter among Negroes. In the campaign of 1888, the Republican National Convention assigned Douglass to cover four key states, among them New York and Michigan. Despite his 70 years, Douglass was on the stump day and night. The victory of the Republicans meant that a federal appointment would be forthcoming, and President Harrison soon named him as Minister-Resident and Consul-General to the Republic of Haiti.

In entering upon his new duties Douglass had fair prospects of success. Ever a hard worker, he would not fail for want of diligence. Moreover when he arrived in Port-au-Prince in early October, 1889, the Haitians welcomed him with open arms, knowing of his career. For 15 months Douglass discharged his duties well, and he had visions of leaving behind a good reputation. But his ministry to Haiti was not destined to end on a happy note. In January, 1891, he became a key figure when the United States announced its intention to seek a naval lease of Môle St. Nicholas, sometimes styled "The Gibraltar of Haiti."

Douglass supported the move, giving no sign if his ardor was somewhat less than that of the State Department. But whatever the enthusiasm of the Americans, it was not shared in the Caribbean.

The Haitian Government, fearful of jeopardizing its sovereignty, and fully aware that its own people were hostile to the lease, politely turned it down. Although not to blame for the failure to obtain the Môle, Douglass was disappointed. This setback, plus his health —he found the tropical heat enervating—led him in June, 1891, to send in his resignation to Secretary of State Blaine. Douglass never held another federal post. The Democrats returned to power in 1892, and President Cleveland was still in office when Douglass died.

His last few years were serene, if indeed not happy. His second marriage had turned out well. Whenever he had occasion to look backward, his thoughts were pleasant and companionable, honors and fame having been his portion. Douglass, however, did not live in the past. He kept busy—speaking, writing, corresponding. Even on his last day—February 20, 1895—he was active. On that afternoon he attended a meeting of the National Council of Women, where he was warmly received as a long-time exponent of the equality of the sexes. He returned home, and as he and his wife were talking after dinner, his heart gave way; before help could be summoned, he was dead.

Nearly two hours later, as the National Council of Women opened their evening session, May Wright Sewall, the presiding officer, took solemn note of his passing. It was a historic coincidence, she said, that the man who embodied the struggle between liberty and oppression should have spent his last day in company with the seekers of "a new expression of freedom." It was a sentiment Douglass would not have quarreled with, being not wide of the mark.

Chronology of the Life of Frederick Douglass[1]

I. "Perpetual Unpaid Toil" (1817?–1840)

1817? Born a slave (exact date unknown) in Talbot County on the Eastern Shore of Maryland.

1825 Sent to Baltimore where he worked as a houseboy and an unskilled laborer.

1833 Sent to St. Michaels in Talbot County and fell out with his master, Thomas Auld ("My master and myself had quite a number of differences").

1834 Hired out to a professional slave breaker, Edward Covey.

1836 Sent to Baltimore after unsuccessful attempt to escape. Put to work in shipyards.

1838 Escaped from slavery by borrowing a Negro sailor's "protection" papers and impersonating him.

II. "Allow Me to Speak Plainly" (1841–1865)

1841 At abolitionist meeting at Nantucket, Massachusetts, asked to speak of his slavery experiences. Was then hired as a full-time antislavery lecturer.

1845 Published his *Narrative of the Life of Frederick Douglass.*

1845–1847 Toured the British Isles, making speeches on abolition of slavery and abstinence from drink.

1847 Moved to Rochester, New York, where he began to publish a reformist weekly, *The North Star.*

1848 Was only man to take a prominent part in the proceedings of the equal rights for women convention held at Seneca Falls, New York, in July, a meeting which formally inaugurated the woman's rights movement in America.

1858 Entertained John Brown for three weeks as a house guest during time when Brown was laying plans for Harpers Ferry raid.

1863 Recruited Negro troops for Union armies.

[1] From Benjamin Quarles, ed., *Narrative of the Life of Frederick Douglass* (Cambridge, Mass.: Belknap Press of Harvard University Press, 1960), pp. xxv–xxvi. Reprinted by permission of the publisher.

1864	Had second White House audience with Lincoln concerning Negro soldiers.

III. "This Struggle Will Go On" (1866–1895)

1866	Led a delegation of Negroes to visit President Johnson to ascertain his views on matters relating to the recently freed slaves.
1870	Was featured speaker at celebrations of the ratification of the Fifteenth Amendment, the greatest of which was held in Baltimore in mid-May.
1876	At Washington, D. C., on April 14 was orator of the day at unveiling of the freedmen's memorial monument to Abraham Lincoln, for which Negroes had raised more than $16,000.
1877	Appointed by President Hayes as United States Marshal for the District of Columbia.
1881	Appointed by President Garfield as Recorder of Deeds for the District of Columbia.
1883	Led the chorus of condemnation of the Supreme Court for declaring unconstitutional the Civil Rights Act of 1875.
1891	Appointed by President Harrison as Minister-Resident and Consul-General to the Republic of Haiti, and Chargé d'Affaires for Santo Domingo.
1895	Died of a heart attack at Washington, D. C., on February 20, upon returning home after speaking at a woman's rights meeting.

DOUGLASS LOOKS AT THE WORLD

A prolific writer, Frederick Douglass lodged into the record a voluminous testimony. Topping the list were his three autobiographies: Narrative of the Life of Frederick Douglass *(1845),* My Bondage and My Freedom *(1855), and* Life and Times of Frederick Douglass *(1881). As a newspaper editor and correspondent and as a contributor to periodicals other than his own, Douglass had need for a ready pen. Moreover, and almost paradoxically, the need for putting his thoughts in writing was intensified by his great abilities as a speaker. A drawing card on the public platform, Douglass felt an obligation to prepare his speeches in detail, leaving little to the inspiration of the moment. The following selections from the Douglass output are representative as to topical content and chronological balance.*

1

Slaves Singing[1]

One of the vivid recollections that Douglass carried from his days in bondage was the singing of his fellow slaves. To him a slave singing, like everything else relating to slavery, was in reality an indictment of the system. In his Narrative, *written when he was 27, he gives his interpretation of the slaves' reason for singing.*

The home plantation of Colonel Lloyd wore the appearance of a country village. All the mechanical operations for all the farms

[1] From Frederick Douglass, *Narrative of the Life of Frederick Douglass* (Boston: Anti-Slavery Office, 1845), pp. 12–15.

were performed here. The shoemaking and mending, the black-smithing, cartwrighting, coopering, weaving, and grain-grinding, were all performed by the slaves on the home plantation. The whole place wore a business-like aspect very unlike the neighboring farms. The number of houses, too, conspired to give it advantage over the neighboring farms. It was called by the slaves the *Great House Farm*. Few privileges were esteemed higher, by the slaves of the out-farms, than that of being selected to do errands at the Great House Farm. It was associated in their minds with greatness. A representative could not be prouder of his election to a seat in the American Congress, than a slave on one of the out-farms would be of his election to do errands at the Great House Farm. They regarded it as evidence of great confidence reposed in them by their overseers; and it was on this account, as well as a constant desire to be out of the field from under the driver's lash, that they esteemed it a high privilege, one worth careful living for. He was called the smartest and most trusty fellow, who had this honor conferred upon him the most frequently. The competitors for this office sought as diligently to please their overseers, as the office-seekers in the polit-ical parties seek to please and deceive the people. The same traits of character might be seen in Colonel Lloyd's slaves, as are seen in the slaves of the political parties.

The slaves selected to go to the Great House Farm, for the monthly allowance for themselves and their fellow-slaves, were peculiarly enthusiastic. While on their way, they would make the dense old woods, for miles around, reverberate with their wild songs, revealing at once the highest joy and the deepest sadness. They would compose and sing as they went along, consulting neither time nor tune. The thought that came up, came out—if not in the word, in the sound;—and as frequently in the one as in the other. They would sometimes sing the most pathetic sentiment in the most rapturous tone, and the most rapturous sentiment in the most pathetic tone. Into all of their songs they would manage to weave something of the Great House Farm. Especially would they do this, when leaving home. They would then sing most exultingly the following words:—

"I am going away to the Great House Farm!
O, yea! O, yea! O!"

This they would sing, as a chorus, to words which to many would seem unmeaning jargon, but which, nevertheless, were full of meaning to themselves. I have sometimes thought that the mere hearing of those songs would do more to impress some minds with the horrible character of slavery, than the reading of whole volumes of philosophy on the subject could do.

I did not, when a slave, understand the deep meaning of those rude and apparently incoherent songs. I was myself within the circle; so that I neither saw nor heard as those without might see and hear. They told a tale of woe which was then altogether beyond my feeble comprehension; they were tones loud, long, and deep; they breathed the prayer and complaint of souls boiling over with the bitterest anguish. Every tone was a testimony against slavery, and a prayer to God for deliverance from chains. The hearing of those wild notes always depressed my spirit, and filled me with ineffable sadness. I have frequently found myself in tears while hearing them. The mere recurrence to those songs, even now, afflicts me; and while I am writing these lines, an expression of feeling has already found its way down my cheek. To those songs I trace my first glimmering conception of the dehumanizing character of slavery. I can never get rid of that conception. Those songs still follow me, to deepen my hatred of slavery, and quicken my sympathies for my brethren in bonds. If any one wishes to be impressed with the soul-killing effects of slavery, let him go to Colonel Lloyd's plantation, and, on allowance day, place himself in the deep pine woods, and there let him, in silence, analyze the sounds that shall pass through the chambers of his soul,—and if he is not thus impressed, it will only be because "there is no flesh in his obdurate heart."

I have often been utterly astonished, since I came to the north, to find persons who could speak of the singing, among slaves, as evidence of their contentment and happiness. It is impossible to conceive of a greater mistake. Slaves sing most when they are most unhappy. The songs of the slave represent the sorrows of his heart; and he is relieved by them, only as an aching heart is relieved by its tears. At least, such is my experience. I have often sung to drown my sorrow, but seldom to express my happiness. Crying for joy, and singing for joy, were alike uncommon to me while in the jaws of slavery. The singing of a man cast away upon a desolate island might be as appropriately considered as evidence of contentment and happiness, as the singing of a slave; the songs of the one and of the other are prompted by the same emotion.

2
A Demanding Overseer[1]

*One of the vivid recollections that Douglass carried
from his days in bondage was the behavior of a slave overseer,
Austin Gore. In his* Narrative, *written when he was 27, Douglass describes Gore's treatment of a slave named Demby. That
this story is true is indicated by the plantation records, which
for the year 1823 carry the simple notation, "Bill Demby
dead."*

Mr. Gore was proud, ambitious, and persevering. He was artful,
cruel, and obdurate. He was just the man for such a place, and it
was just the place for such a man. It afforded scope for the full
exercise of all his powers, and he seemed to be perfectly at home
in it. He was one of those who could torture the slightest look,
word, or gesture, on the part of the slave, into impudence, and
would treat it accordingly. There must be no answering back to
him; no explanation was allowed a slave, showing himself to have
been wrongfully accused. Mr. Gore acted fully up to the maxim
laid down by slaveholders,—"It is better that a dozen slaves suffer
under the lash, than that the overseer should be convicted, in the
presence of the slaves, of having been at fault." No matter how
innocent a slave might be—it availed him nothing, when accused
by Mr. Gore of any misdemeanor. To be accused was to be convicted, and to be convicted was to be punished; the one always following the other with immutable certainty. To escape punishment
was to escape accusation; and few slaves had the fortune to do
either, under the overseership of Mr. Gore. He was just proud
enough to demand the most debasing homage of the slave, and

[1] From Frederick Douglass, *Narrative of the Life of Frederick Douglass* (Boston: Anti-Slavery Office, 1845), pp. 45–48.

quite servile enough to crouch, himself, at the feet of the master.
He was ambitious enough to be contented with nothing short of
the highest rank of overseers, and persevering enough to reach the
height of his ambition. He was cruel enough to inflict the severest
punishment, artful enough to descend to the lowest trickery, and
obdurate enough to be insensible to the voice of a reproving conscience. He was, of all the overseers, the most dreaded by the slaves.
His presence was painful; his eye flashed confusion; and seldom
was his sharp, shrill voice heard, without producing horror and
trembling in their ranks.

Mr. Gore was a grave man, and, though a young man, he in-
dulged in no jokes, said no funny words, seldom smiled. His words
were in perfect keeping with his looks, and his looks were in perfect keeping with his words. Overseers will sometimes indulge in a
witty word, even with the slaves; not so with Mr. Gore. He spoke
but to command, and commanded but to be obeyed; he dealt spar-
ingly with his words, and bountifully with his whip, never using
the former where the latter would answer as well. When he
whipped, he seemed to do so from a sense of duty, and feared no
consequences. He did nothing reluctantly, no matter how disagree-
able; always at his post, never inconsistent. He never promised but
to fulfill. He was, in a word, a man of the most inflexible firmness
and stone-like coolness.

His savage barbarity was equalled only by the consummate coolness with which he committed the grossest and most savage deeds
upon the slaves under his charge. Mr. Gore once undertook to
whip one of Colonel Lloyd's slaves, by the name of Demby. He had
given Demby but few stripes, when, to get rid of the scourging, he
ran and plunged himself into a creek, and stood there at the depth
of his shoulders, refusing to come out. Mr. Gore told him that he
would give him three calls, and that, if he did not come out at the
third call, he would shoot him. The first call was given. Demby
made no response, but stood his ground. The second and third
calls were given with the same result. Mr. Gore then, without
consultation or deliberation with any one, not even giving Demby
an additional call, raised his musket to his face, taking deadly aim
at his standing victim, and in an instant poor Demby was no more.

His mangled body sank out of sight, and blood and brains marked the water where he had stood.

A thrill of horror flashed through every soul upon the plantation, excepting Mr. Gore. He alone seemed cool and collected. He was asked by Colonel Lloyd and my old master, why he resorted to this extraordinary expedient. His reply was (as well as I can remember) that Demby had become unmanageable. He was setting a dangerous example to the other slaves,—one which, if suffered to pass without some such demonstration on his part, would finally lead to the total subversion of all rule and order upon the plantation. He argued that if one slave refused to be corrected, and escaped with his life, the other slaves would soon copy the example; the result of which would be, the freedom of the slaves, and the enslavement of the whites. Mr. Gore's defence was satisfactory. He was continued in his station as overseer upon the home plantation. His fame as an overseer went abroad. His horrid crime was not even submitted to judicial investigation. It was committed in the presence of slaves, and they of course could neither institute a suit, nor testify against him; and thus the guilty perpetrator of one of the bloodiest and most foul murders goes unwhipped of justice, and uncensured by the community in which he lives. Mr. Gore lived in St. Michael's, Talbot county, Maryland, when I left there; and if he is still alive, he very probably lives there now; and if so, he is now, as he was then, as highly esteemed and as much respected as though his guilty soul had not been stained with his brother's blood.

3
Praying with His Legs[1]

Bent on escape from slavery, Douglass made his dream a reality in September, 1838. The exact manner of his escape, however, he did not reveal until after the Civil War. In an article for The Century Magazine *in 1881, Douglass described his escape and his reasons for withholding the details so long.*

In the first narrative of my experience in slavery, written nearly forty years ago, and in various writings since, I have given the public what I considered very good reasons for withholding the manner of my escape. In substance these reasons were, first, that such publication at any time during the existence of slavery might be used by the master against the slave, and prevent the future escape of any who might adopt the same means that I did. The second reason was, if possible, still more binding to silence: the publication of details would certainly have put in peril the persons and property of those who assisted. Murder itself was not more sternly and certainly punished in the State of Maryland than . . . aiding and abetting the escape of a slave. Many colored men, for no other crime than that of giving aid to a fugitive slave, have, like Charles T. Torrey, perished in prison. The abolition of slavery in my native State and throughout the country, and the lapse of time, render the caution hitherto observed no longer necessary. But even since the abolition of slavery, I have sometimes thought it well enough to baffle curiosity by saying that while slavery existed there were good reasons for not telling the manner of my escape, and since slavery had ceased to exist, there was no reason for telling it. I shall

[1] From Frederick Douglass, "My Escape from Slavery," *The Century Magazine,* I (November, 1881), 124–31.

now, however, cease to avail myself of this formula, and, as far as I can, endeavor to satisfy this very natural curiosity. I should, perhaps, have yielded to that feeling sooner, had there been anything very heroic or thrilling in the incidents connected with my escape, for I am sorry to say I have nothing of that sort to tell; and yet the courage that could risk betrayal and the bravery which was ready to encounter death, if need be, in pursuit of freedom, were essential features in the undertaking. My success was due to address rather than courage, to good luck rather than bravery. My means of escape were provided for me by the very men who were making laws to hold and bind me more securely in slavery.

It was the custom in the State of Maryland to require the free colored people to have what were called free papers. These instruments they were required to renew very often, and by charging a fee for this writing, considerable sums from time to time were collected by the State. In these papers the name, age, color, height, and form of the freeman were described, together with any scars or other marks upon his person which could assist in his identification. This device in some measure defeated itself—since more than one man could be found to answer the same general description. Hence many slaves could escape by personating the owner of one set of papers; and this was often done as follows: a slave, nearly or sufficiently answering the description set forth in the papers, would borrow or hire them till by means of them he could escape to a free State, and then, by mail or otherwise, would return them to the owner. The operation was a hazardous one for the lender as well as for the borrower. A failure on the part of the fugitive to send back the papers would imperil his benefactor, and the discovery of the papers in possession of the wrong man would imperil both the fugitive and his friend. It was, therefore, an act of supreme trust on the part of a freeman of color thus to put in jeopardy his own liberty that another might be free. It was, however, not unfrequently bravely done, and was seldom discovered. I was not so fortunate as to resemble any of my free acquaintances sufficiently to answer the description of their papers. But I had one friend—a sailor—who owned a sailor's protection, which answered somewhat the purpose of free papers—describing his person and certifying to the fact that he was a free American sailor. The instrument had at its head the American eagle, which gave it the appearance at once of an authorized document. This protection, when in my hands, did not describe its bearer very accurately. Indeed, it called for a man much darker than myself, and close examination of it would have caused my arrest at the start.

In order to avoid this fatal scrutiny on the part of railroad officials, I arranged with Isaac Rolls, a Baltimore hackman, to bring my baggage to the Philadelphia train just on the moment of starting, and jumped upon the car myself when the train was in motion. Had I gone into the station and offered to purchase a ticket, I should have been instantly and carefully examined, and undoubtedly arrested. In choosing this plan I considered the jostle of the train, and the natural haste of the conductor, in a train crowded with passengers, and relied upon my skill and address in playing the sailor, as described in my protection, to do the rest. One element in my favor was the kind feeling which prevailed in Baltimore and other sea-ports at the time, toward "those who go down to the sea in ships." "Free trade and sailors' rights" just then expressed the sentiment of the country. In my clothing I was rigged out in sailor style. I had on a red shirt and a tarpaulin hat, and a black cravat tied in sailor fashion carelessly and loosely about my neck. My knowledge of ships and sailor's talk came much to my assistance, for I knew a ship from stem to stern, and from keelson to cross-trees, and could talk sailor like an "old salt." I was well on the way to Havre de Grace before the conductor came into the Negro car to collect tickets and examine the papers of his black passengers. This was a critical moment in the drama. My whole future depended upon the decision of this conductor. Agitated though I was while this ceremony was proceeding, still, externally, at least, I was apparently calm and self-possessed. He went on with his duty— examining several colored passengers before reaching me. He was somewhat harsh in tone and peremptory in manner until he reached me, when, strange enough, and to my surprise and relief, his whole manner changed. Seeing that I did not readily produce my free papers, as the other colored persons in the car had done, he said to me, in friendly contrast with his bearing toward the others:

"I suppose you have your free papers?"

To which I answered:

"No, sir; I never carry my free papers to sea with me."

"But you have something to show that you are a freeman, haven't you?"

"Yes, sir," I answered; "I have a paper with the American eagle on it, and that will carry me around the world."

With this I drew from my deep sailor's pocket my seaman's protection, as before described. The merest glance at the paper satisfied him, and he took my fare and went on about his business. This moment of time was one of the most anxious I ever experienced. Had the conductor looked closely at the paper, he could not have failed to discover that it called for a very different-looking person from myself, and in that case it would have been his duty to arrest me on the instant, and send me back to Baltimore from the first station. When he left me with the assurance that I was all right, though much relieved, I realized that I was still in great danger: I was still in Maryland, and subject to arrest at any moment. I saw on the train several persons who would have known me in any other clothes, and I feared they might recognize me, even in my sailor "rig," and report me to the conductor, who would then subject me to a closer examination, which I knew well would be fatal to me.

Though I was not a murderer fleeing from justice, I felt perhaps quite as miserable as such a criminal. The train was moving at a very high rate of speed for that epoch of railroad travel, but to my anxious mind it was moving far too slowly. Minutes were hours, and hours were days during this part of my flight. After Maryland, I was to pass through Delaware—another slave State, where slave-catchers generally awaited their prey, for it was not in the interior of the State, but on its borders, that these human hounds were most vigilant and active. The border lines between slavery and freedom were the dangerous ones for the fugitives. The heart of no fox or deer, with hungry hounds on his trail in full chase, could have beaten more anxiously or noisily than did mine from the time I left Baltimore till I reached Philadelphia. The passage of the Susquehanna River at Havre de Grace was at that time made by ferry-boat, on board of which I met a young colored man by the name of Nichols, who came very near betraying me. He was a "hand" on the boat, but, instead of minding his business, he insisted upon knowing me, and asking me dangerous questions as to where I was going, when I was coming back, etc. I got away from my old and inconvenient acquaintance as soon as I could decently do so, and went to another part of the boat. Once across the river, I encountered a new danger. Only a few days before, I had been at work on a revenue cutter, in Mr. Price's ship-yard in Baltimore, under the care of Captain McGowan. On the meeting at this point of the two trains, the one going south stopped on the track just opposite to the one going north, and it so happened that this Captain McGowan sat at a window where he could see me very distinctly, and would certainly have recognized me had he looked at me but for a second. Fortunately, in the hurry of the moment, he did not see me; and the trains soon passed each other on their respective ways. But this was not my only hair-breadth escape. A German blacksmith whom I knew well was on the train with me, and looked at me very intently, as if he thought he had seen me somewhere before in his travels. I really believe he knew me, but had no heart to betray me. At any rate, he saw me escaping and held his peace.

The last point of imminent danger, and the one I dreaded most, was Wilmington. Here we left the train and took the steam-boat for Philadelphia. In making the change here I again apprehended arrest, but no one disturbed me, and I was soon on the broad and beautiful Delaware, speeding away to the Quaker City. On reaching Philadelphia in the afternoon, I inquired of a colored man how I could get on to New York. He directed me to the William-street depot, and thither I went, taking the train that night. I reached New York Tuesday morning, having completed the journey in less than twenty-four hours.

My free life began on the third of September, 1838. On the morning of the fourth of that month, after an anxious and most perilous but safe journey, I found myself in the big city of New York, a *free man*—one more added to the mighty throng which, like the confused waves of the troubled sea, surged to and fro between the lofty walls of Broadway. Though dazzled with the wonders which met me on every hand, my thoughts could not be much withdrawn from my strange situation. For the moment, the dream of my youth and the hopes of my manhood were completely fulfilled. The bonds that had held me to "old master" were broken. No man now had a right to call me his slave or assert mastery over me. I was in the rough and tumble of an outdoor world, to take my chance with the rest of its busy number. I have often been asked how I felt when first I found myself on free soil. There is scarcely anything in my experience about which I could not give a more satisfactory answer. A new world had opened upon me. If life is more than breath and the "quick round of blood," I lived more in that one day than in a year of my slave life. It was a time of joyous excitement which words can but tamely describe. In a letter written to a friend soon after reaching New York, I said: "I felt as one might feel upon escape from a den of hungry lions." Anguish and grief, like darkness and rain, may be depicted; but gladness and joy, like the rainbow, defy the skill of pen or pencil. During ten or fifteen years I had been, as it were, dragging a heavy chain which no strength of mine could break; I was not only a slave, but a slave for life. I might become a husband, a father, an aged man, but through all, from birth to death, from the cradle to the grave, I had felt myself doomed. All efforts I had previously made to secure my freedom had not only failed, but had seemed only to rivet my fetters the more firmly, and to render my escape more difficult. Baffled, entangled, and discouraged, I had at times asked myself the question, May not my condition after all be God's work, and ordered for a wise purpose, and if so, is not submission my duty? A contest had in fact been going on in my mind for a long time, between the clear consciousness of right and the plausible make-shifts of theology and superstition. The one held me an abject slave—a prisoner for life, punished for some transgression in which I had no lot nor part; and the other counseled me to manly endeavor to secure my freedom. This contest was now ended; my chains were broken, and the victory brought me unspeakable joy.

4

Message to the British[1]

As a free man Douglass took a keen interest in the abolition movement, becoming an abolitionist lecturer in 1841. After four years of touring up and down New England, Douglass decided to go to the British Isles. He expected to draw large and sympathetic audiences, and he was not disappointed. His tour of nearly 20 months was climaxed by a well-attended reception at the London Tavern on March 30, 1847, arranged by the British abolitionists, headed by George Thompson, a member of Parliament. Douglass's long address, constantly interrupted by loud cheers, reveals the eloquent style and hard-hitting content that characterized his abolitionist speeches. It might be added that the efforts of Douglass and other Negro Americans did much to strengthen British reformist sentiment.

I never stood before an audience like that I now see before me without feeling my incompetence to do justice to the cause which I am here to advocate, or to the expectation which is generally created for me by the friends who precede me. Certainly, if the eulogiums bestowed upon me this evening were correct, I should be able to entertain this audience for hours by my eloquence; but I claim none of this. While I feel grateful for the generosity of my friends, I can certainly claim very little right to their applause, for I was once a slave. I never had a day's schooling in my life: all that I know I have stolen (*cheers*), and I wish at once to relieve you from all expectation of a great speech. That I am deeply and earnestly engaged in advocating the cause of my brethren is most

[1] From *Report of Proceedings at the Soiree Given to Frederick Douglass, London Tavern, March 30, 1847* (London: R. Yorke Clarke and Co., 1847), pp. 15–19, 28–29.

true, and as such, this evening, I hail your kind expressions towards me with the profoundest gratitude. I will make use of these expressions; I will take them home in my memory, they shall be written upon my heart, and I will use them in that land of boasted liberty and light, yet that land of abject slavery, for the purpose of overthrowing that system, and restoring the Negro to his long lost rights. Sir, the time for argument on this question is over; but place me in an assembly of ministers or of politicians who call in question my right to freedom, and I can stand up and open my mouth, and assert boldly and strongly my rights; but where all is admitted, where almost every one is waiting for the last word of a sentiment, that he may cheer it for the end of the most radical resolution, that he may hold up his hand in favour of it—I certainly have very little to do. You have done all for me. Still, sir, I may manage, perhaps out of the scraps you have left, to make a coat of many colours; which, for the reasons stated, I must request you to receive with indulgence.

I have listened to the patriotic, or, rather, the respectful language used towards America and towards Americans. I confess that, although I am going back to that country, though I have many friends there, I am not here to make any professions of respect whatever to that country, or to its institutions. The fact is, the whole system —the whole network of American Society—is one great falsehood. Americans have become dishonest men from the very circumstances by which they are surrounded. Seventy years ago they went to the battle-field in defence of liberty. Sixty years ago they formed a Constitution, over the very gateway of which they inscribed, "To secure the blessings of liberty to ourselves and our posterity!" In their Declaration of Independence they made the loudest and clearest assertions of the rights of man; at the very same time, the men who draw up the Declaration of Independence—the very men who framed the American Constitution—the very men who adopted that Constitution—were trafficking in the bodies and souls of their fellow-men. From the adoption of the Constitution of the United States downwards, everything good and great in the heart of the American people, everything patriotic, has been summoned to defend that great lie before the world; they have been driven from their very patriotism to defend this great falsehood. How have they done it? They have done so by wrapping slavery up in honied words, and calling it our "peculiar institution," our "social system," our "patriarchal institution," our "democratic institution." They have spoken of it in every way but the right way. In their Constitution, no less than three clauses may be found of the most determined hostility to the liberty of the black in that country; yet clothed in such language that no Englishman could take offence at it; for instance, the President of the United States "shall, at all times, and in all cases, call out the army and navy to suppress domestic insurrections." The Englishman in reading that clause of the Constitution, would very readily assent to the justice of this proposition. The army and navy, what is it good for, but to suppress insurrection, and preserve the quiet and harmony of society? But, what does it mean as shadowed forth in that Constitution—what does it mean to the Americans? It means this—every man who casts a ball in the American ballot, becomes that very man who raises his hand in support of the American Constitution. Every man who swears to support that instrument, at the same time swears that slaves of that country shall be slaves or die. This clause of the Constitution converts every American into an enemy of the black man in that land. Every bayonet, every sword, every musket, and every cannon has its deadly aim at the bosom of the Negro. Three millions of them lie there under the heel of seventeen millions of white men. There each one stands, with all the means of co-operation, there they stand sworn before God and the universe that the slaves shall be slaves or die.

Take another clause of the American Constitution. "No person, held to service or labor, in any state, under the laws thereof, if taken into another shall, in consequence of any law or regulation therein, be released from such service or labor; but shall be delivered up on claim of the party to whom such service or labor may be due."

Upon the face of this, there is nothing of injustice, nothing of inhumanity; it is perfectly in accordance with justice, perfectly humane; it is indeed just what it *should* be according to your notions of things, and the general use of words. But what does it mean in the United States? It means that if any slave shall in the darkness of midnight, thinking himself a man, and entitled to the rights of a man, steal away from the hovel or quarter, shall snap the chain that binds his leg, shall break the fetter that links him to slavery, and seek a refuge from a democracy by flying to a monarchy, that that slave in all his windings, by night and by day, on his way from a land of slavery to one of freedom, shall be liable to be hunted down like a felon and dragged back to the bondage from which he has escaped. So that this clause of the Constitution is one of the greatest safeguards to that slave system which we have met here this evening to express our detestation of. This clause of the Constitution makes that whole land one vast hunting ground for man. This clause of the Constitution gives to the slave-holder the right, any moment to set his blood-hound, well trained, upon the track of his fugitive, hunt him down and drag him back to the jaws of slavery, to the master from whom he had escaped. This clause of the Constitution consecrates every rood of earth in that land over which the star-spangled banner waves, *slave hunting ground*. There is no valley so deep, no mountain so high, no plain so extensive, no spot so sacred, throughout that whole land, as to enable a man having a skin like mine to enjoy the right to his own hand. He will, if he escape, be hunted down in a moment. You know in the Mosaic economy, to which reference has been made by a preceding speaker, we hear there the command given as it were amid thunder and lightning in Sinai, "Thou shalt not deliver unto his master the servant that has escaped; he shall dwell in the place, thou shalt not oppress him." America has run into the very face of Jehovah, and has said, Thou *shalt* deliver unto his master, thou *shalt* deliver unto the tyrant who usurps authority over his fellow-man, the trembling bondman who escapes. This clause of the Constitution is one of the most deadly kind, one that, more than all other clauses, serves to keep up that system of fraud and inhumanity that is now crushing millions, identified with me by their complexions, in their chains. The slave-holders of the south would be wholly unable to hold the slaves but for the existence of these safeguards, but for these the slaves would run away; they do not love their masters so well as their masters flatter themselves. They *do* frequently run away, you have an instance of it before you (*great cheering*). The northern states stand round the slave system; they say to the slave-holder, "We have a sentiment, we have a feeling of abhorrence against slavery, we would not hold slaves ourselves. We are sincerely opposed to slavery, but if any of your slaves venture to run away from you and come among us we will return them to you, and while you can make them believe that, of course they will not run away. Besides if your slaves attempt to gain their freedom by force, we will bring down upon them the whole civil, military, and naval force of the nation, and crush them into obedience. Tell them that we will do so, and we will give them every evidence that we *will*, by our votes in Congress, by our religious assemblies, by our deadly hate, by our fierce prejudice against the colored man; if he dares to attempt to gain his freedom we kill him. Yet let it be understood that we hate slavery *(laughter)*." This being the state of things in America, I cannot be very patriotic, I hope you will not expect any very eloquent outbursts of eulogy or praises of America from me on this occasion. No my friends, I am going to be honest with America; I am going to the United States soon, but I go there to do as I have done here, —to unmask her pretensions to republicanism,—to unmask her hypocritical pretensions to Christianity,—to denounce her pretensions to civilization,—to proclaim in her ear the wrongs of those who cry day and night to heaven, "How long, how long, oh Lord God!" *(sensation)*. I go to that land with no flattery, no flummery about her greatness; she is great in territory, she may boast of broad lakes, of mighty rivers, she is great in her enterprise, she is great in intellectual sagacity, she is great in her history; but, Sir, while I remember that with her broadest lakes and with her finest rivers, the tears and blood of my brethren are mingled and forgotten, I cannot speak well of her principles, I cannot eulogise her institutions. She is unworthy, she stands there upon the quivering heart-strings of three millions of people. She punishes the black man for crimes for which she allows the white man to escape. She declares on her statute book that the black man shall be seventy times more liable to the punishment of death than the white man. In the state of Virginia there are seventy-one crimes for which a black man may be punished with death, only one of which crimes will subject a white man to that penalty *(cries of "shame")*. She will not allow her black population to meet together and worship God according to the dictates of their own consciences; if they meet more than seven of them together for the purpose of worshipping God, or for the purpose of improving their minds in any shape or form, each one of them may be taken according to law and whipped nine and thirty lashes upon their bare backs, and burned with a red-hot iron (*loud cries of shame*)! If any one of them shall be found riding a horse, be it by day or night, he may be taken and whipped forty lashes on his bare back, his ear cropped, and his cheek branded with a red-hot iron (*shame, shame*). In all the slave states of the south they make it a crime punishable with severe fines, and imprisonment in many cases, to instruct the slave to read the pages of inspired wisdom. In the state of Mississippi, a man is liable to a heavy fine for teaching a slave to read. In the state of Alabama for the third offence in teaching a slave to read, it is death. In the state of Louisiana, the second offence is punishable with death. In the state of South Carolina it is death by the law to aid a slave in escaping from a brutal owner. If a woman in defence of her own person, her own dignity as a woman, against the brutal and infernal designs of a determined master, raises a hand in her defence, she may be legally put to death upon the spot (*loud and indignant cries of "shame"*). Sir, I cannot speak of such a nation as this with any degree of respect, especially when that nation is loud and long in its boasts of holy liberty and life (*cries of "no, no"*)! When upon the wings of the press she is hurling her denunciations at the despotisms of Europe,—when she embraces every opportunity to scorn and scoff at this government, and to taunt and to denounce you as all slaves and as bowing under a haughty monarchy,—when she is stamping on her every coin, from the cent to the dollar, from the dollar to the eagle, the sacred name of liberty,—when upon every hill may be seen erected the pole bearing the liberty cap, under which waves the star-spangled banner,—when upon every fourth day of July we hear declarations like this, "Oh! God, we thank thee that we live in a land of religious and civil liberty,"—when from the platform of the orator on that day we hear the boast, "ours is a glorious land,"—I say, when such professions as these are put forth to the world, I have not a word of patriotic regard to offer. This nation presents to the world an anomaly that no other nation does present. They are the boldest in their pretensions, the oldest in their profession of the love of freedom; yet no nation on the globe can present

a statute book so full of all that is cruel, of all that is malicious, of
all that is infernal, as the American statute book (*hear, hear*). Every
page is red with the blood of the oppressed American slave.

One of our own poets says,—

> "What! mothers from their children riven,
>   What! God's own image bought and sold;
> *Americans* to market driven,
>   And bartered like the brute for gold."

. . . Thus is slavery ensconced at this moment. The abolitionists
thus seeing slavery woven, and interwoven, with the net-work of our
civil and religious organization, have resolved, at whatever hazard
—at the hazard of reputation, of ease, of comfort, of luxury, or of
life, they have resolved to pursue it; to illustrate my meaning, they
have adopted the motto of Pat in a Tipperary row, "Wherever you
see a head, hit it" (*laughter*). Wherever slavery manifests itself in the
United States the abolitionists will hit it; they will deal out their
blows at it. They have followed it from the street to the church, and
the church to the pulpit, for slavery affects to be very pious, very
devotional, disposed to pray, the moment we touch it. It goes to
church, kneels down, and prays, and when we come to rebuke it,
"You are an infidel," and straightway some press in this land takes
up the cry. The clamor is got up not against the slave-holder, but
against the man who is virtuously laboring for the overthrow of that
system. The clamor is got up not in favor of the slave, but against
the abolitionist, against his only friend. When the history of the
abolition movement shall have been fairly written, it will be found
that the abolitionists were the men in the nineteenth century, who
dared to defend the Bible from the blasphemous charge of sanction-
ing and sanctifying Negro slavery (*cheers*). It will be found that they
were the men who dared to stand up and demand that churches,
calling themselves by Christian names, should utterly and for ever
purify themselves from all contact, all connection, all fellowship with
men, who gained their fortunes by the blood of souls. It will be
found that they were the men who cried aloud and spared not; who
lifted up their voices like trumpets against the giant iniquities by
which they were surrounded; it will be found they were the men

planting themselves on the immutable, the eternal, and all-compre-
hensive principle of the sacred New Testament, "All things what-
soever ye would that men should do unto you, do ye even so unto
them." They, acting upon this principle, feeling that if the fetters
were on their own limbs, if the chain was on their own person, if
the lash was falling quick and heavy upon their own quivering flesh,
they would desire their fellow-men to be faithful in their behalf;
they, acting on this principle, have dared to risk their lives, their
fortunes, their honor, and their all, for the purpose of rescuing from
the tyrannous grasp of the slave-holder those three millions of tram-
pled down slaves. . . .

I have now been in this country nineteen months, I have travelled
through the length and breadth of it; I came here a slave, I came
here degraded, I came here under a load of odium heaped upon my
race by the American press, by the American pulpit, by the American people: I have gone through this land and I have steadily increased, I may say, although I speak it of myself, I have steadily
increased the amount of attention bestowed upon this question by
the British people. Wherever I have gone I have been treated with
the utmost kindness, with the utmost deference, with the utmost attention. I have reason to love England. Truly liberty in England is
better than slavery in America; liberty in a monarchy, is better than
despotism in democracy; freedom at Hyde Park corner is better than
slavery in front of the American capital. I have known then these
last nineteen months what it was, for the first time in my life, to
enjoy freedom. Just before leaving Boston for this country, I was
not allowed even to ride in a public conveyance; I was kicked from
an omnibus. I was driven from the lower floor of a church, because
I had dared to enter there, forgetting my complexion, remembering
that I was a man, and thinking that I had an interest in the gospel
there proclaimed. In my passage to this country, I was driven out of
the cabin of the steam boat, out of all respectable parts of the ship,
on to the floor of the deck, among the cattle—not allowed to take
my place among human beings as a man and a brother. I was not
allowed to go into a menagerie or a theatre, if I wanted to go, nor to
a museum, nor into an athenæum, nor into a portrait gallery if I
wished to do so. I was not allowed any of these privileges: I was
mobbed, I was beaten, I was driven, dragged, insulted, outraged,

in all directions: every white man, no matter how black his heart, could insult me with impunity. I came to this land—how great the change! The moment I stepped upon the soil at Liverpool, I saw people as white as any I ever saw in the United States, as noble in their exterior, and instead of seeing the curled lip of scorn, the fire of hate kindled in the eye of the Englishman, all was respect and kindness (*cheers*). I looked round in vain for the insult; I looked, for I hardly believed my eyes; I searched to see if I could see in an Englishman any look of disapprobation of me on account of my complexion—not one (*hearty cheers*). I have travelled in all parts of the country, in Ireland, in Scotland, and in England and Wales; I have travelled upon highways, byeways, railways, and steam boats, and in none of these instances have I met with anything that I could torture into an expression of disrespect of me on account of my complexion (*loud cheers*). I have visited your Colosseum, your museum, your gallery of paintings; I even had the pleasure of going into your House of Commons, and still more, into the House of Lords, and of hearing what I never heard before, and what I had long wished to hear, the eloquence of Lord Brougham (*cheers*). In none of these places did I receive one word of scorn. I have felt, however much Americans may despise and affect to scorn the Negro, that Englishmen—the best of Englishmen, do not hesitate to give the right hand of manly fellowship to such as I am (*much cheering*). When I return to the United States I will try to impress them with these facts, and to shame them into a sense of decency upon this subject. Why, Sir, the Americans do not know that I am a man; they think the Negro is something between the man and the monkey. The very dogs here, Sir, know that I am a man. I was at a public meeting at Bromley the other day, and while I was speaking, a great Newfoundland dog came and put his paws on the platform, and gazed up at me with such interest, that I could tell, by the very expression of his eye, that he recognized my humanity (*general laughter*).

I came here a slave, but I go back free. I came here despised, I go back with a reputation. For I am sure that if the Americans will believe one tithe of all that has been said in this country respecting me, they will certainly admit that I am better than I was. Though in better circumstances than I came, yet I go back to toil, not to have ease and comfort. Since I came to this land I have had every inducement to stop here. The kindness of my friends in the north has been unbounded; they have proffered me every inducement to bring my family over into this country, they have even gone so far as to offer to give money that they might be brought to this land, and I should settle down here in a different position from that I should occupy in the United States; but I prefer to live a life of activity, I prefer to go home, to go back to America. I glory in the conflict, that I may also glory in the victory. I go back, turning away from the ease and respectability which I might maintain here, I go back for the sake of my brethren (*cheers*), I go back to suffer with them, to toil with them, to endure insult with them, to speak for them, to write for them, to struggle in the ranks with them, for that emancipation, which is yet to be achieved by the power of truth over the basest selfishness (*great cheering*). I go back gladly. I leave this country for the United States on the 4th of April, which is near at hand. I feel not merely satisfied, but highly gratified, with my visit to this country.

I will tell my colored countrymen how Englishmen feel for them. It will be something to give them patience under their sorrows, and hope of a future emancipation. I shall try to have daguerreotyped upon my heart this sea of upturned faces. I will tell them this; it will strengthen them in their sufferings and in their toils; and I am sure in this I shall have your sympathy, as well as their blessing. Pardon me, my friends, for the disconnected manner in which I have addressed you, but I have spoken out of the fulness of my heart; as the words came up, so have they been uttered; not altogether, perhaps, so delicately, systematically, and refinedly as they might have been, but still you must take them as they are. They are the free outgushings of my heart, overborne with grateful emotion for the kindness I have received in this country, from the day I arrived here, to the present moment. With deepest gratitude, farewell.

5

No Day of Triumph[1]

The Fourth of July evoked no enthusiasm among abolitionists; they held that it was inconsistent to celebrate independence and freedom in a land in which slavery existed. Douglass shared this view, preferring to let the day pass in silence. However, when he was invited by the Rochester Ladies' Anti-Slavery Society to deliver the Fourth of July oration in 1852, he made the most of the occasion. His speech was not devoted to patriotic themes but addressed itself to the question, "What, to the American slave, is your Fourth of July?"

The papers and placards say that I am to deliver a Fourth of July Oration. This certainly sounds large, and out of the common way, for me. It is true that I have often had the privilege to speak in this beautiful Hall, and to address many who now honor me with their presence. But neither their familiar faces, nor the perfect gage I think I have of Corinthian Hall seems to free me from embarrassment.

The fact is, ladies and gentlemen, the distance between this platform and the slave plantation, from which I escaped, is considerable —and the difficulties to be overcome in getting from the latter to the former are by no means slight. That I am here to-day is, to me, a matter of astonishment as well as of gratitude. You will not, therefore, be surprised, if in what I have to say I evince no elaborate preparation, nor grace my speech with any high sounding exordium. With little experience and with less learning, I have been able to throw my thoughts hastily and imperfectly together; and trusting to your patient and generous indulgence, I will proceed to lay them before you.

[1] From *Oration, Delivered in Corinthian Hall, Rochester, by Frederick Douglass, July 5, 1852* (Rochester: Lee, Mann and Company, 1852), pp. 3–5, 14–15, 20, 32–35, 37–39.

This, for the purpose of this celebration, is the Fourth of July. It is the birthday of your National Independence, and of your political freedom. This, to you, is what the Passover was to the emancipated people of God. It carries your minds back to the day, and to the act of your great deliverance; and to the signs, and to the wonders, associated with that act, and that day. This celebration also marks the beginning of another year of your national life; and reminds you that the Republic of America is now 76 years old. I am glad, fellow-citizens, that your nation is so young. Seventy-six years, though a good old age for a man, is but a mere speck in the life of a nation. Three score years and ten is the allotted time for individual men; but nations number their years by thousands. According to this fact, you are, even now, only in the beginning of your national career, still lingering in the period of childhood. I repeat, I am glad this is so. There is hope in the thought, and hope is much needed, under the dark clouds which lower above the horizon. The eye of the reformer is met with angry flashes, portending disastrous times; but his heart may well beat lighter at the thought that America is young, and that she is still in the impressible stage of her existence. May he not hope that high lessons of wisdom, of justice and of truth, will yet give direction to her destiny? Were the nation older, the patriot's heart might be sadder, and the reformer's brow heavier. Its future might be shrouded in gloom, and the hope of its prophets go out in sorrow. There is consolation in the thought that America is young. —Great streams are not easily turned from channels, worn deep in the course of ages. They may sometimes rise in quiet and stately majesty, and inundate the land, refreshing and fertilizing the earth with their mysterious properties. They may also rise in wrath and fury, and bear away, on their angry waves, the accumulated wealth of years of toil and hardship. They, however, gradually flow back to the same old channel, and flow on as serenely as ever. But, while the river may not be turned aside, it may dry up, and leave nothing behind but the withered branch, and the unsightly rock, to howl in the abyss-sweeping wind, the sad tale of departed glory. As with rivers so with nations. . . .

Fellow-citizens, pardon me, allow me to ask, why am I called upon to speak here to-day? What have I, or those I represent, to do with your national independence? Are the great principles of political freedom and of natural justice, embodied in that Declaration of Independence, extended to us? and am I, therefore, called upon to bring our humble offering to the national altar, and to confess the benefits and express devout gratitude for the blessings resulting from your independence to us?

Would to God, both for your sakes and ours, that an affirmative answer could be truthfully returned to these questions! Then would my task be light, and my burden easy and delightful. For *who* is there so cold, that a nation's sympathy could not warm him? Who so obdurate and dead to the claims of gratitude, that would not thankfully acknowledge such priceless benefits? Who so stolid and selfish, that would not give his voice to swell the hallelujahs of a nation's jubilee, when the chains of servitude had been torn from his limbs? I am not that man. In a case like that, the dumb might eloquently speak, and the "lame man leap as an hart."

But such is not the state of the case. I say it with a sad sense of the disparity between us. I am not included within the pale of this glorious anniversary! Your high independence only reveals the immeasurable distance between us. The blessings in which you, this day, rejoice, are not enjoyed in common.—The rich inheritance of justice, liberty, prosperity and independence, bequeathed by your fathers, is shared by you, not by me. The sunlight that brought light and healing to you, has brought stripes and death to me. This Fourth of July is *yours,* not *mine. You* may rejoice, *I* must mourn. To drag a man in fetters into the grand illuminated temple of liberty, and call upon him to join you in joyous anthems, were inhuman mockery and sacrilegious irony. Do you mean, citizens, to mock me, by asking me to speak to-day? If so, there is a parallel to your conduct. And let me warn you that it is dangerous to copy the example of a nation whose crimes, towering up to heaven, were thrown down by the breath of the Almighty, burying that nation in irrevocable ruin! I can to-day take up the plaintive lament of a peeled and woe-smitten people! . . .

What, to the American slave, is your 4th of July? I answer; a day that reveals to him, more than all other days in the year, the gross injustice and cruelty to which he is the constant victim. To him, your celebration is a sham; your boasted liberty, an unholy license; your national greatness, swelling vanity; your sounds of rejoicing are empty and heartless; your denunciation of tyrants, brass fronted impudence; your shouts of liberty and equality, hollow mockery; your prayers and hymns, your sermons and thanksgivings, with all your religious parade and solemnity, are, to him, mere bombast, fraud, deception, impiety, and hypocrisy—a thin veil to cover up crimes which would disgrace a nation of savages. There is not a nation on the earth guilty of practices more shocking and bloody than are the people of the United States, at this very hour.

Go where you may, search where you will, roam through all the monarchies and despotisms of the Old World, travel through South America, search out every abuse, and when you have found the last, lay your facts by the side of the everyday practices of this nation, and you will say with me, that, for revolting barbarity and shameless hypocrisy, America reigns without a rival. . . .

Americans! your republican politics, not less than your republican religion, are flagrantly inconsistent. You boast of your love of liberty, your superior civilization, and your pure Christianity, while the whole political power of the nation (as embodied in the two great political parties) is solemnly pledged to support and perpetuate the enslavement of three millions of your countrymen. You hurl your anathemas at the crowned headed tyrants of Russia and Austria and pride yourselves on your Democratic institutions, while you yourselves consent to be the mere *tools* and *body-guards* of the tyrants of Virginia and Carolina. You invite to your shores fugitives of oppression from abroad, honor them with banquets, greet them with ovations, cheer them, toast them, salute them, protect them, and pour out your money to them like water; but the fugitives from your own land you advertise, hunt, arrest, shoot, and kill. You glory in your refinement and your universal education; yet you maintain a system as barbarous and dreadful as ever stained the character of a nation —a system begun in avarice, supported in pride, and perpetuated in cruelty. You shed tears over fallen Hungary, and make the sad story of her wrongs the theme of your poets, statesmen, and orators, till your gallant sons are ready to fly to arms to vindicate her cause against the oppressor; but, in regard to the ten thousand wrongs of the American slave, you would enforce the strictest silence, and would hail him as an enemy of the nation who dares to make those wrongs the subject of public discourse! You are all on fire at the mention of liberty for France or for Ireland; but are as cold as an iceberg at the thought of liberty for the enslaved of America. You discourse eloquently on the dignity of labor; yet, you sustain a system which, in its very essence, casts a stigma upon labor. You can bare your bosom to the storm of British artillery to throw off a three-penny tax on tea; and yet wring the last hard earned farthing from the grasp of the black laborers of your country. You profess to believe "that, of one blood, God made all nations of men to dwell on the face of all the earth," and hath commanded all men, everywhere, to love one another; yet you notoriously hate (and glory in your hatred) all men whose skins are not colored like your own. You declare before the world, and are understood by the world to declare that you *"hold these truths to be self-evident, that all men are created equal; and are endowed by their Creator with certain inalienable rights; and that among these are, life, liberty, and the pursuit of happiness";* and yet, you hold securely, in a bondage which, according to your own Thomas Jefferson, *"is worse than ages of that which your fathers rose in rebellion to oppose," a seventh part* of the inhabitants of your country.

Fellow-citizens, I will not enlarge further on your national inconsistencies. The existence of slavery in this country brands your republicanism as a sham, your humanity as a base pretense, and your Christianity as a lie. It destroys your moral power abroad: it corrupts your politicians at home. It saps the foundation of religion; it makes your name a hissing and a bye-word to a mocking earth. It is the antagonistic force in your government, the only thing that seriously disturbs and endangers your *Union.* It fetters your progress; it is the enemy of improvement; the deadly foe of education; it fosters pride; it breeds insolence; it promotes vice; it shelters crime; it is a curse to the earth that supports it; and yet you cling to it as if it were the sheet anchor of all your hopes. Oh! be warned! be warned! a horrible reptile is coiled up in your nation's bosom; the venomous creature is nursing at the tender breast of your youthful republic; *for the love of God, tear away,* and fling from you the hideous monster, and *let the weight of twenty millions crush and destroy it forever!* . . .

Allow me to say, in conclusion, notwithstanding the dark picture I have this day presented, of the state of the nation, I do not despair of this country. There are forces in operation which must inevitably work the downfall of slavery. "The arm of the Lord is not shortened," and the doom of slavery is certain. I, therefore, leave off where I began, with hope. While drawing encouragement from "the Declaration of Independence," the great principles it contains, and the genius of American Institutions, my spirit is also cheered by the obvious tendencies of the age. Nations do not now stand in the same relation to each other that they did ages ago. No nation can now shut itself up from the surrounding world and trot round in the same old path of its fathers without interference. The time was when such could be done. Long established customs of hurtful character could formerly fence themselves in, and do their evil work with social impunity. Knowledge was then confined and enjoyed by the privileged few, and the multitude walked on in mental darkness. But a change has now come over the affairs of mankind. Walled cities and empires have become unfashionable. The arm of commerce has borne away the gates of the strong city. Intelligence is penetrating the darkest corners of the globe. It makes its pathway over and under the sea, as well as on the earth. Wind, steam, and lightning are its chartered agents. Oceans no longer divide, but link nations together. From Boston to London is now a holiday excursion. Space is comparatively annihilated. Thoughts expressed on one side of the Atlantic are distinctly heard on the other.

The far off and almost fabulous Pacific rolls in grandeur at our feet. The Celestial Empire, the mystery of ages, is being solved. The fiat of the Almighty, "Let there be Light," has not yet spent its force. No abuse, no outrage whether in taste, sport or avarice, can now hide itself from the all-pervading light. The iron shoe, and crippled foot of China must be seen in contrast with nature. Africa must rise and put on her yet unwoven garment. "Ethiopia shall stretch out her hand unto God." In the fervent aspirations of William Lloyd Garrison, I say, and let every heart join in saying it:

God speed the year of jubilee
The wide world o'er!

6
The Job Ceiling[1]

Not content with denouncing slavery, Douglass gave much attention to bettering the lot of the Negro already free. Job discrimination was the most important hurdle facing the Negro in the North. He was generally unable to find jobs other than those which were unskilled, poorly paid, and unsteady. Since 1830, Negro leaders had stressed the necessity for better jobs, for making the colored worker proficient in the mechanic arts. Douglass became a leading exponent of skilled labor for the Negro, urging it in his newspaper, such as in the editorial "Learn Trades or Starve," appearing in Frederick Douglass' Paper *for March 4, 1853. Four days later he expressed himself more fully in a letter to Harriet Beecher Stowe, which won her support, although later she withdrew it. This letter was made a part of the official record of the colored convention of 1853, held in Rochester in July, 1853, where Douglass had read it so that his colleagues might know the exact nature of his representation to Mrs. Stowe. The letter also appears in* Frederick Douglass' Paper, *December 2, 1853.*

You kindly informed me, when at your house, a fortnight ago, that you designed to do something which should permanently contribute to the improvement and elevation of the free colored people in the United States. You especially expressed an interest in such of this class as had become free by their own exertions, and desired most of all to be of service to them. In what manner, and by what means, you can assist this class most successfully, is the subject upon which you have done me the honor to ask my opinion.

Begging you to excuse the unavoidable delay, I will now most

[1] From *Proceedings of the Colored National Convention Held in Rochester, July 6th, 7th and 8th, 1853* (Rochester: Office of F. Douglass' Paper, 1853), pp. 33–38.

gladly comply with your request, but before doing so, I desire to express, dear Madam, my deep sense of the value of the services which you have already rendered my afflicted and persecuted people, by the publication of your inimitable book on the subject of slavery. That contribution to our bleeding cause, alone, involves us in a debt of gratitude which cannot be measured; and your resolution to make other exertions on our behalf excites in me emotions and sentiments, which I scarcely need try to give forth in words. Suffice it to say, that I believe you do have the blessings of your enslaved countrymen and countrywomen; and the still higher reward which comes to the soul in the smiles of our merciful Heavenly father, whose ear is ever open to the cries of the oppressed.

With such sentiments, dear Madam, I will at once proceed to lay before you, in as few words as the nature of the case will allow, my humble views in the premises. First of all, let me briefly state the nature of the disease, before I undertake to prescribe the remedy. Three things are notoriously true of us as a people. These are POV-ERTY, IGNORANCE AND DEGRADATION. Of course there are exceptions to this general statement; but these are so few as only to prove its essential truthfulness. I shall not stop here to inquire minutely into the causes which have produced our present condition; nor to denounce those whom I believe to be responsible for these causes. It is enough that we shall agree upon the character of the evil, whose existence we deplore, and upon some plan for its removal.

I assert then, that *poverty, ignorance* and *degradation* are the com-bined evil or, in other words, these constitute the social disease of the Free Colored people in the United States.

To deliver them from this triple malady, is to improve and ele-vate them, by which I mean simply to put them on an equal footing with their white fellow-countrymen in the sacred right to *"Life, Liberty* and the pursuit of happiness."* I am for no fancied or arti-ficial elevation, but only ask fair play. How shall this be obtained? I answer, first, not by establishing for our use high schools and col-leges. Such institutions are, in my judgment, beyond our immediate occasions, and are not adapted to our present most pressing wants. High schools and colleges are excellent institutions, and will, in due season, be greatly subservient to our progress; but they are the result, as well as they are the demand of a point of progress, which we, as a people, have not yet attained. Accustomed, as we have been, to the rougher and harder modes of living, and of gaining a livelihood, we cannot, and we ought not to hope that, in a single leap from our low condition, we can reach that of *Ministers, Lawyers, Doctors, Editors, Merchants,* &c. These will, doubtless, be attained by us; but this will only be, when we have patiently and laboriously, and I may add successfully, mastered and passed through the intermediate gradations of agriculture and the mechanic arts. Besides, there are (and perhaps this is a better reason for my view of the case) numerous institutions of learning in this country, already thrown open to colored youth. To my thinking, there are quite as many facilities now afforded to the colored people, as they can spare the time, from the sterner duties of life, to avail themselves of. In their present condition of poverty, they cannot spare their sons and daughters two or three years of boarding schools or colleges, to say nothing of finding the means to sustain them while at such institutions. I take it, therefore, that we are well provided for in this respect; and that it may be fairly inferred from the past that the facilities for our education, so far as schools and colleges in the Free States are concerned, will increase quite in proportion with our future wants. Colleges have been open to colored youth in this country during the last dozen years. Yet few, comparatively, have acquired a classical education; and even this few have found themselves educated far above a living condition, there being no methods by which they could turn their learning to account. Several of this latter class have entered the ministry; but you need not be told that an educated people is needed to sustain an educated ministry. There must be a certain amount of cultivation among the people to sustain such a ministry. At present, we have not that cultivation amongst us; and therefore, we value, in the preacher, strong lungs, rather than high learning. I do not say that educated ministers are not needed amongst us.—Far from it! I wish there were more of them; but to increase their number is *not* the largest benefit you can bestow upon us.

You, dear Madam, can help the masses. You can do something for the thousands; and by lifting these from the depths of poverty and ignorance, you can make an educated ministry and an educated class possible. In the present circumstances, prejudice is a bar to the

educated black minister among the whites; and ignorance is a bar
to him among the blacks.

We have now two or three colored lawyers in this country; and I
rejoice in the fact; for it affords very gratifying evidence of our progress. Yet it must be confessed that, in point of success, our lawyers
are as great failures as are our ministers. White people will not
employ them to the obvious embarrassment of their causes, and the
blacks, taking their *cue* from the whites, have not sufficient confidence in their abilities to employ them. Hence, educated colored
men, among the colored people, are at a very great discount. It
would seem that education and emigration go together with us; for
as soon as a man rises amongst us, capable, by his genius and learning, to do us great service, just so soon he finds that he can serve
himself better by going elsewhere. In proof of this, I might instance
the Russwurms—the Garnetts—the Wards—the Crummells and
others—all men of superior ability and attainments, and capable of
removing mountains of prejudice against their race, by their simple
presence in the country; but these gentlemen, finding themselves
embarrassed here by the peculiar disadvantages to which I have
referred—disadvantages in part growing out of their education—
being repelled by ignorance on the one hand, and prejudice on the
other, and having no taste to continue a contest against such odds,
they have sought more congenial climes, where they can live more
peaceable and quiet lives. I regret their election—but I cannot
blame them; for, with an equal amount of education, and the hard
lot which was theirs, I might follow their example.

But, again, it has been said that the colored people must become
farmers—that they must go on the land, in order to their elevation.
Hence, many benevolent people are contributing the necessary funds
to purchase land in Canada, and elsewhere, for them. That prince
of good men, Gerrit Smith, has given away thousands of acres to
colored men in this State, thinking, doubtless, that in so doing he
was conferring a blessing upon them. Now, while I do not under-
value the efforts which have been made, and are still being made in
this direction, yet I must say that I have far less confidence in such
efforts, than I have in the benevolence which prompts them. Agricultural pursuits are not, as I think, suited to our condition. The
reason of this is not to be found so much in the occupation (for

it is a noble and ennobling one), as in the people themselves. That is only a remedy, which can be applied to the case; and the difficulty in agricultural pursuits, as a remedy for the evils of poverty and ignorance amongst us, is that it cannot, for various reasons, be applied.

We cannot apply it, because it is almost impossible to get colored men to go on the land. From some cause or other (perhaps the adage that misery loves company will explain), colored people will congregate in the large towns and cities; and they will endure any amount of hardship and privation, rather than separate, and go into the country. Again, very few have the means to set up for themselves, or to get where they could do so.

Another consideration against expending energy in this direction is our want of self-reliance. Slavery more than all things else, robs its victims of self-reliance. To go into the western wilderness, and there to lay the foundation of future society, requires more of that important quality than a life of slavery has left us. This may sound strange to you, coming as it does from a colored man; but I am dealing with facts, and these never accommodate themselves to the feelings or wishes of any. They don't *ask,* but *take leave to be.* It is a fact then, and not less so because I wish it were otherwise, that the colored people are wanting in self-reliance—too fond of society —too eager for immediate results—and too little skilled in mechanics or husbandry to attempt to overcome the wilderness; at least, until they have overcome obstacles less formidable. Therefore, I look to other means than agricultural pursuits for the elevation and improvement of colored people. Of course, I allege this of the many. There are exceptions. Individuals among us, with commendable zeal, industry, perseverance and self-reliance, have found, and are finding, in agricultural pursuits, the means of supporting, improving and educating their families.

The plan which I contemplate will (if carried into effect), greatly increase the number of this class—since it will prepare others to meet the rugged duties which a pioneer agricultural condition must impose upon all who take it upon them. What I propose is intended simply to prepare men for the work of getting an honest living— not out of dishonest men—but out of an honest earth.

Again, there is little reason to hope that any considerable number of the free colored people will ever be induced to leave this country, even if such a thing were desirable. This black man—*un*like the Indian—loves civilization. He does not make very great progress in civilization himself but he likes to be in the midst of it, and prefers to share its most galling evils, to encountering barbarism. Then the love of the country, the dread of isolation, the lack of adventurous spirit, and the thought of seeming to desert their "brethren in bonds," are a powerful check upon all schemes of colonization which look to the removal of the colored people, without the slaves. The truth is, dear Madam, we are *here,* and here we are likely to remain. Individuals emigrate—nations never. We have grown up with this republic, and I see nothing in her character, or even in the character of the American people as yet, which compels the belief that we must leave the United States. If then, we are to remain here, the question for the wise and good is precisely that you have submitted to me—namely: What can be done to improve the condition of the free people of color in the United States? The plan which I humbly submit in answer to this inquiry—and in the hope that it may find favor with you, and with many friends of humanity who honor, love and co-operate with you—is the establishment in Rochester, N. Y., or in some other part of the United States equally favorable to such an enterprise, of an Industrial College in which shall be taught several important branches of the mechanical arts. This college is to be opened to colored youth. I will pass over, for the present, the details of such an institution as I propose. It is not worth while that I should dwell upon these at all. Once convinced that something of the sort is needed, and the organizing power will be forthcoming. It is the peculiarity of your favored race that they can always do what they think necessary to be done. I can safely trust all details to yourself, and the wise and good people whom you represent in the interest you take in my oppressed fellow-countrymen.

Never having had a day's schooling in all my life I may not be expected to map out the details of a plan so comprehensive as that involved in the idea of a college. I repeat, then, I leave the organization and administration to the superior wisdom of yourself and the friends who second your noble efforts. The argument in favor of an Industrial College—a college to be conducted by the best men—

and the best workmen which the mechanical arts can afford; a college where colored youth can be instructed to use their hands, as well as their heads; where they can be put into possession of the means of getting a living whether their lot in after life may be cast among civilized or uncivilized men; whether they choose to stay here, or prefer to return to the land of their fathers—is briefly this: prejudice against the free colored people in the United States has shown itself nowhere so invincible as among mechanics. The farmer and the professional man cherish no feeling so bitter as that cherished by these. The latter would starve us out of the country entirely. At this moment I can more easily get my son into a lawyer's office to learn law than I can into a blacksmith's shop to blow the bellows and to wield the sledge-hammer. Denied the means of learning useful trades we are pressed into the narrowest limits to obtain a livelihood. In times past we have been the hewers of wood and the drawers of water for American society, and we once enjoyed a monopoly in the menial enjoyments, but this is so no longer. Even these enjoyments are rapidly passing away out of our hands. The fact is—every day begins with the lesson, and ends with the lesson —the colored men must learn trades; and must find new employment; new modes of usefulness to society, or that they must decay under the pressing wants to which their condition is rapidly bringing them.

We must become mechanics; we must build as well as live in houses; we must make as well as use furniture; we must construct bridges as well as pass over them, before we can properly live or be respected by our fellow men. We need mechanics as well as ministers. We need workers in iron, clay, and leather. We have orators, authors, and other professional men, but these reach only a certain class, and get respect for our race in certain select circles. To live here as we ought we must fasten ourselves to our countrymen through their every day cardinal wants. We must not only be able to *black* boots, but to *make* them. At present we are unknown in the Northern States as mechanics. We give no proof of genius or skill at the county, State, or national fairs. We are unknown at any of the great exhibitions of the industry of our fellow-citizens, and being unknown we are unconsidered.

The fact that we make no show of our ability is held conclusive of our inability to make any, hence all the indifference and contempt with which incapacity is regarded, fall upon us, and that too, when we have had no means of disproving the infamous opinion of our natural inferiority. I have during the last dozen years denied before the Americans that we are an inferior race; but this has been done by arguments based upon admitted principles rather than by the presentation of facts. Now, firmly believing, as I do, that there are skill, invention, power, industry, and real mechanical genius, among the colored people, which will bear favorable testimony for them, and which only need the means to develop them, I am decidedly in favor of the establishment of such a college as I have mentioned. The benefits of such an institution would not be confined to the Northern States, nor to the free colored people. They would extend over the whole Union. The slave not less than the freeman would be benefited by such an institution. It must be confessed that the most powerful argument now used by the Southern slaveholder, and the one most soothing to his conscience, is that derived from the low condition of the free colored people of the North. I have long felt that too little attention has been given by our truest friends in this country to removing this stumbling block out of the way of the slave's liberation.

The most telling, the most killing refutation of slavery, is the presentation of an industrious, enterprising, thrifty, and intelligent free black population. Such a population I believe would rise in the Northern States under the fostering care of such a college as that supposed.

To show that we are capable of becoming mechanics I might adduce any amount of testimony; dear madam, I need not ring the charges on such a proposition. There is no question in the mind of any unprejudiced person that the Negro is capable of making a good mechanic. Indeed, even those who cherish the bitterest feelings towards us have admitted that the apprehension that Negroes might be employed in their stead, dictated the policy of excluding them from trades altogether. But I will not dwell upon this point as I fear I have already trespassed too long upon your precious time, and written more than I ought to expect you to read. Allow me to say in conclusion, that I believe every intelligent colored man in America will approve and rejoice at the establishment of some such institution as that now suggested. There are many respectable colored men, fathers of large families, having boys nearly grown up, whose minds are tossed by day and by night with the anxious enquiry, "what shall I do with my boys?" Such an institution would meet the wants of such persons. Then, too, the establishment of such an institution would be in character with the eminently practical philanthropy of your trans-Atlantic friends. America could scarce object to it as an attempt to agitate the public mind on the subject of slavery, or to *dissolve the Union*. It could not be tortured into a cause for hard words by the American people, but the noble and good of all classes, would see in the effort an excellent motive, a benevolent object, temperately, wisely, and practically manifested.

7

The Dred Scott Decision[1]

No measure by a branch of the federal government ever angered abolitionists and Negroes as did the Dred Scott decision. This ruling by the Supreme Court permitted slavery in the territories, thereby strengthening it. As if that were not enough, the decision also stripped the Negro of his claim to citizenship. The decision was bitterly denounced, and in the chorus of condemnation no language was stronger than that of Douglass as delivered in a speech on May 14, 1857, before an abolitionist gathering.

While four millions of our fellow countrymen are in chains —while men, women, and children are bought and sold on the auction-block with horses, sheep, and swine—while the remorseless slave-whip draws the warm blood of our common humanity—it is meet that we assemble as we have done to-day, and lift up our hearts and voices in earnest denunciation of the vile and shocking abomination. It is not for us to be governed by our hopes or our fears in this great work; yet it is natural on occasions like this, to survey the position of the great struggle which is going on between slavery and freedom, and to dwell upon such signs of encouragement as may have been lately developed, and the state of feeling these signs or events have occasioned in us and among the people generally. It is a fitting time to take an observation to ascertain where we are, and what our prospects are.

To many, the prospects of the struggle against slavery seem far from cheering. Eminent men, North and South, in Church and State, tell us that the omens are all against us. Emancipation, they

[1] From *Two Speeches by Frederick Douglass: One on West India Emancipation, and the Other on the Dred Scott Decision* (Rochester: C. P. Dewey, 1857), pp. 27–35, 46.

tell us, is a wild, delusive idea; the price of human flesh was never higher than now; slavery was never more closely entwined about the hearts and affections of the southern people than now; that whatever of conscientious scruple, religious conviction, or public policy, which opposed the system of slavery forty or fifty years ago, has subsided; and that slavery never reposed upon a firmer basis than now. Completing this picture of the happy and prosperous condition of this system of wickedness, they tell us that this state of things is to be set to our account. Abolition agitation has done it all. How deep is the misfortune of my poor, bleeding people, if this be so! How lost their condition, if even the efforts of their friends but sink them deeper in ruin!

Without assenting to this strong representation of the increasing strength and stability of slavery, without denouncing what of untruth pervades it, I own myself not insensible to the many difficulties and discouragements that beset us on every hand. They fling their broad and gloomy shadows across the pathway of every thoughtful colored man in this country. For one, I see them clearly, and feel them sadly. With an earnest, aching heart, I have long looked for the realization of the hope of my people. Standing, as it were, barefoot, and treading upon the sharp and flinty rocks of the present, and looking out upon the boundless sea of the future, I have sought, in my humble way, to penetrate the intervening mists and clouds, and, perchance, to descry, in the dim and shadowy distance, the white flag of freedom, the precise speck of time at which the cruel bondage of my people should end, and the long entombed millions rise from the foul grave of slavery and death. But of that time I can know nothing, and you can know nothing. All is uncertain at that point. One thing, however, is certain; slaveholders are in earnest, and mean to cling to their slaves as long as they can, and to the bitter end. They show no sign of a wish to quit their iron grasp upon the sable throats of their victims. Their motto is, "a firmer hold and a tighter grip" for every new effort that is made to break their cruel power. The case is one of life or death with them, and they will give up only when they must do that or do worse.

In one view the slaveholders have a decided advantage over all opposition. It is well to notice this advantage—the advantage of complete organization. They are organized; and yet were not at the pains of creating their organizations. The State governments, where the system of slavery exists, are complete slavery organizations. The church organizations in those States are equally at the service of slavery; while the Federal Government, with its army and navy, from the chief magistracy in Washington, to the Supreme Court, and thence to the chief marshalship at New York, is pledged to support, defend, and propagate the crying curse of human bondage. The pen, the purse, and the sword, are united against the simple truth, preached by humble men in obscure places.

This is one view. It is, thank God, only one view; there is another, and a brighter view. David, you know, looked small and insignificant when going to meet Goliath, but looked larger when he had slain his foe. . . . Thus hath it ever been. Oppression, organized as ours is, will appear invincible up to the very hour of its fall. Sir, let us look at the other side, and see if there are not some things to cheer our heart and nerve us up anew in the good work of emancipation.

Take this fact—for it is a fact—the anti-slavery movement has, from first to last, suffered no abatement. It has gone forth in all directions, and is now felt in the remotest extremities of the Republic.

It started small, and was without capital either in men or money. The odds were all against it. It literally had nothing to lose, and every thing to gain. There was ignorance to be enlightened, error to be combatted, conscience to be awakened, prejudice to be overcome, apathy to be aroused, the right of speech to be secured, mob violence to be subdued, and a deep, radical change to be inwrought in the mind and heart of the whole nation. This great work, under God, has gone on, and gone on gloriously.

Amid all changes, fluctuations, assaults, and adverses of every kind, it has remained firm in its purpose, steady in its aim, onward and upward, defying all opposition, and never losing a single battle. Our strength is in the growth of anti-slavery conviction, and this has never halted.

There is a significant vitality about this abolition movement. It has taken a deeper, broader, and more lasting hold upon the national heart than ordinary reform movements. Other subjects of much interest come and go, expand and contract, blaze and vanish, but the huge question of American Slavery, comprehending, as it does, not merely the weal or the woe of four millions, and their countless posterity, but the weal or the woe of this entire nation, must increase in magnitude and in majesty with every hour of its history. From a cloud not bigger than a man's hand, it has over-spread the heavens. It has risen from a grain not bigger than a mustard seed. Yet see the fowls of the air, how they crowd its branches.

Politicians who cursed it, now defend it; ministers, once dumb, now speak in its praise; and presses, which once flamed with hot denunciations against it, now surround the sacred cause as by a wall of living fire. Politicians go with it as a pillar of cloud by day, and the press as a pillar of fire by night. With these ancient tokens of success, I, for one, will not despair of our cause.

Those who have undertaken to suppress and crush out this agitation for liberty and humanity, have been most woefully dis-appointed. Many who have engaged to put it down, have found themselves put down. The agitation has pursued them in all their meanderings, broken in upon their seclusion, and, at the very moment of fancied security, it has settled down upon them like a mantle of unquenchable fire. Clay, Calhoun, and Webster each tried his hand at suppressing the agitation; and they went to their graves disappointed and defeated.

Loud and exultingly have we been told that the slavery question is settled, and settled forever. You remember it was settled thirty-seven years ago, when Missouri was admitted into the Union with a slaveholding constitution, and slavery prohibited in all territory north of thirty-six degrees of north latitude. Just fifteen years after-wards, it was settled again by voting down the right of petition, and gagging down free discussion in Congress. Ten years after this it was settled again by the annexation of Texas, and with it the war with Mexico. In 1850 it was again settled. This was called a final settlement. By it slavery was virtually declared to be the equal of liberty, and should come into the Union on the same terms. By it the right and the power to hunt down men, women, and children, in every part of this country, was conceded to our southern brethren, in order to keep them in the Union. Four years after this settlement, the whole question was once more settled, and settled by a settlement which unsettled all the former settlements.

The fact is, the more the question has been settled, the more it has needed settling. The space between the different settlements has been strikingly on the decrease. The first stood longer than any of its successors.

There is a lesson in these decreasing spaces. The first stood fifteen years—the second, ten years—the third, five years—the fourth stood four years—and the fifth has stood the brief space of two years.

This last settlement must be called the Taney settlement. We are now told, in tones of lofty exultation, that the day is lost—all lost— and that we might as well give up the struggle. The highest authority has spoken. The voice of the Supreme Court has gone out over the troubled waves of the National Conscience, saying peace, be still.

This infamous decision of the Slaveholding wing of the Supreme Court maintains that slaves are within the contemplation of the Constitution of the United States, property; that slaves are property in the same sense that horses, sheep, and swine are property; that the old doctrine that slavery is a creature of local law is false; that the right of the slaveholder to his slave does not depend upon the local law, but is secured wherever the Constitution of the United States extends; that Congress has no right to prohibit slavery anywhere; that slavery may go in safety anywhere under the star-spangled banner; that colored persons of African descent have no rights that white men are bound to respect; that colored men of African descent are not and cannot be citizens of the United States.

You will readily ask me how I am affected by this devilish decision—this judicial incarnation of wolfishness? My answer is, and no thanks to the slaveholding wing of the Supreme Court, my hopes were never brighter than now.

I have no fear that the National Conscience will be put to sleep by such an open, glaring, and scandalous tissue of lies as that decision is, and has been, over and over, shown to be.

The Supreme Court of the United States is not the only power in this world. It is very great, but the Supreme Court of the Almighty is greater. Judge Taney can do many things, but he cannot perform impossibilities. He cannot bail out the ocean, annihilate this firm old earth, or pluck the silvery star of liberty from our Northern sky. He may decide, and decide again; but he cannot reverse the decision of the Most High. He cannot change the essential nature of things—making evil good, and good, evil.

Happily for the whole human family, their rights have been defined, declared, and decided in a court higher than the Supreme Court. "There is a law," says Brougham, "above all the enactments of human codes, and by that law, unchangeable and eternal, man cannot hold property in man."

Your fathers have said that man's right to liberty is self-evident. There is no need of argument to make it clear. The voices of nature, of conscience, of reason, and of revelation, proclaim it as the right of all rights, the foundation of all trust, and of all responsibility. Man was born with it. It was his before he comprehended it. The *deed* conveying it to him is written in the centre of his soul, and is recorded in Heaven. The sun in the sky is not more palpable to the sight than man's right to liberty is to the moral vision. To decide against this right in the person of Dred Scott, or the humblest and most whip-scarred bondman in the land, is to decide against God. It is an open rebellion against God's government. It is an attempt to undo what God has done, to blot out the broad distinction instituted by the *Allwise* between men and things, and to change the image and superscription of the everliving God into a speechless piece of merchandise.

Such a decision cannot stand. God will be true though every man be a liar. We can appeal from this hell-black judgment of the Supreme Court, to the court of common sense and common humanity. We can appeal from man to God. If there is no justice on earth, there is yet justice in heaven. You may close your Supreme Court against the black man's cry for justice, but you cannot, thank God, close against him the ear of a sympathising world, nor shut up the Court of Heaven. All that is merciful and just, on earth and in Heaven, will execrate and despise this edict of Taney.

If it were at all likely that the people of these free States would tamely submit to this demoniacal judgment, I might feel gloomy and sad over it, and possibly it might be necessary for my people to look for a home in some other country. But as the case stands, we have nothing to fear.

In one point of view, we, the abolitionists and colored people, should meet this decision, unlooked for and monstrous as it appears, in a cheerful spirit. This very attempt to blot out forever the hopes of an enslaved people may be one necessary link in the chain of events preparatory to the downfall, and complete overthrow of the whole slave system.

The whole history of the anti-slavery movement is studded with proof that all measures devised and executed with a view to allay and diminish the anti-slavery agitation, have only served to increase, intensify, and embolden that agitation. This wisdom of the crafty has been confounded, and the counsels of the ungodly brought to nought. It was so with the Fugitive Slave Bill. It was so with the Kansas Nebraska Bill; and it will be so with this last and most shocking of all pro-slavery devices, this Taney decision.

When great transactions are involved, where the fate of millions is concerned, where a long enslaved and suffering people are to be delivered, I am superstitious enough to believe that the finger of the Almighty may be seen bringing good out of evil, and making the wrath of man redound to his honor, hastening the triumph of righteousness.

The American people have been called upon, in a most striking manner, to abolish and put away forever the system of slavery. The subject has been pressed upon their attention in all earnestness and sincerity. The cries of the slave have gone forth to the world, and up to the throne of God. This decision, in my view, is a means of keeping the nation awake on the subject. It is another proof that God does not mean that we shall go to sleep, and forget that we are a slaveholding nation.

Step by step we have seen the slave power advancing; poisoning, corrupting, and perverting the institutions of the country; growing more and more haughty, imperious, and exacting. The white man's liberty has been marked out for the same grave with the black man's.

The ballot box is desecrated, God's law set at nought, armed legislators stalk the halls of Congress, freedom of speech is beaten down in the Senate. The rivers and highways are infested by border ruffians, and white men are made to feel the iron heel of slavery.

This ought to arouse us to kill off the hateful thing. They are solemn warnings to which the white people, as well as the black people, should take heed.

If these shall fail, judgment, more fierce or terrible, may come. The lightning, whirlwind, and earthquake may come. Jefferson said that he trembled for his country when he reflected that God is just, and his justice cannot sleep forever. The time may come when even the crushed worm may turn under the tyrant's feet. Goaded by cruelty, stung by a burning sense of wrong, in an awful moment of depression and desperation, the bondman and bondwoman at the South may rush to one wild and deadly struggle for freedom. Already slaveholders go to bed with bowie knives, and apprehend death at their dinners. Those who enslave, rob, and torment their cooks, may well expect to find death in their dinner-pots.

The world is full of violence and fraud, and it would be strange if the slave, the constant victim of both fraud and violence, should escape the contagion. He, too, may learn to fight the devil with fire, and for one, I am in no frame of mind to pray that this may be long deferred. . . .

By all the laws of nature, civilization, and of progress, slavery is a doomed system. Not all the skill of politicians, North and South, not all the sophistries of Judges, not all the fulminations of a corrupt press, not all the hypocritical prayers, or the hypocritical refusals to pray of a hollow-hearted priesthood, not all the devices of sin and Satan, can save the vile thing from extermination. . . .

I base my sense of the certain overthrow of slavery, in part, upon the nature of the American Government, the Constitution, the tendencies of the age, and the character of the American people; and this, notwithstanding the important decision of Judge Taney.

I know of no soil better adapted to the growth of reform than American soil. I know of no country where the conditions for effecting great changes in the settled order of things, for the development of right ideas of liberty and humanity, are more favorable than here in these United States.

The very groundwork of this government is a good repository of Christian civilization. The Constitution, as well as the Declaration of Independence, and the sentiments of the founders of the Republic, give us a platform broad enough, and strong enough, to

support the most comprehensive plans for the freedom and elevation of all the people of this country, without regard to color, class,
or clime. . . .

The Constitution knows all the human inhabitants of this country as "the people." It makes, as I have said before, no discrimination in favor of, or against, any class of the people, but is fitted to
protect and preserve the rights of all, without reference to color,
size, or any physical peculiarities. Besides, it has been shown by
William Goodell and others, that in eleven out of the old thirteen
States, colored men were legal voters at the time of the adoption of
the Constitution.

In conclusion, let me say, all I ask of the American people is,
that they live up to the Constitution, adopt its principles, imbibe
its spirit, and enforce its provisions.

When this is done, the wounds of my bleeding people will be
healed, the chain will no longer rust on their ankles, their backs
will no longer be torn by the bloody lash, and liberty, the glorious
birthright of our common humanity, will become the inheritance
of all the inhabitants of this highly favored country.

8

Douglass and John Brown[1]

Inevitably two such militants as Douglass and John Brown would not go unacquainted. Their first meeting went back to 1848, 11 years before the raid on Harpers Ferry, when Douglass visited Brown in Springfield, Massachusetts, in response to his invitation. This visit ripened into a friendship, climaxed in early 1858, when Brown spent five weeks in Rochester as a house guest of the Douglass family. Hence when Brown was seized for leading a raid on the government arsenal at Harpers Ferry on October 16, 1859, Douglass, as a known friend, was in danger of being implicated as an accomplice. To avoid seizure by federal authorities, Douglass hastened to Canada. Safe on foreign soil, he realized that his flight was hardly heroic, however sensible. He was given an opportunity to explain his role when John E. Cook, one of the men taken at Harpers Ferry, charged him with having failed to keep his promise to furnish the Brown raiders with additional men and weapons on the eve of the coup. Making the most of this obviously false accusation, Douglass wrote a letter (subsequently widely reprinted) to a Rochester newspaper.

LETTER FROM FREDERICK DOUGLASS

Canada West, Monday, Oct. 31, 1859.

To the Editor of the Rochester Democrat:

I notice that the telegram makes Mr. Cook (one of the unfortunate insurgents at Harpers Ferry, and now a prisoner in the hands of the thing calling itself the Government of Virginia, but which is but an organized conspiracy by one party of the people against the other and weaker) denounce me as a coward—and so assert that I prom-

---

[1] From *The Anglo-African Magazine* (New York), December, 1859, pp. 381–82.

ised to be present in person at the Harpers Ferry insurrection. This is certainly a very grave impeachment, whether viewed in its bearings upon friends or upon foes, and you will not think it strange that I should take a somewhat serious notice of it. Having no acquaintance whatever with Mr. Cook, and never having exchanged a word with him about the Harpers Ferry insurrection, I am disposed to doubt that he could have used the language concerning me which the wires attributed to him. The lightning, when speaking for itself, is among the most direct, reliable and truthful of things; but when speaking for the terror-stricken slave-holders at Harpers Ferry it has been made the swiftest of liars. Under their nimble and trembling fingers it magnified seventeen men into seven hundred— and has since filled the columns of the New York Herald for days with interminable contradictions. But assuming that it has told the truth as to the sayings of Mr. Cook in this instance, I have this answer to make to my accuser: Mr. Cook may be perfectly right in denouncing me as a coward. I have not one word to say in defense or vindication of my character for courage. I have always been more distinguished for running than fighting—and tried by the Harpers Ferry insurrection test, I am most miserably deficient in courage— even more so than Cook, when he deserted his brave old Captain and fled to the mountains. To this extent Mr. Cook is entirely right, and will meet no contradiction from me or from anybody else. But wholly, grievously and most unaccountably wrong is Mr. Cook, when he asserts that I promised to be present in person at the Harpers Ferry insurrection. Of whatever other imprudence and indiscretion I may have been guilty, I have never made a promise so rash and wild as this. The taking of Harpers Ferry was a measure never encouraged by my word or by my vote, at any time or place. My wisdom, or my cowardice, has not only kept me from Harpers Ferry, but has equally kept me from making any promise to go there. I desire to be quite emphatic here—for all guilty men he is the guiltiest who lures his fellow men to an undertaking of this sort, under promise of assistance, which he afterwards fails to render. I therefore declare that there is no man living, and no man dead, who, if living, could truthfully say that I ever promised him or anybody else, either conditionally or otherwise, that I would be present in person at the Harpers Ferry insurrection. My field of

labor for the abolition of Slavery has not extended to an attack
upon the United States Arsenal. In the teeth of the documents already published, and of those which may hereafter be published, I
affirm that no man connected with that insurrection, from its noble
and heroic leader down, can connect my name with a single broken
promise of any sort whatever. So much I may deem it proper to say
negatively.

*The time for a full statement of what I know, and of all I know,
of this desperate but sublimely disinterested effort to emancipate
the slaves of Maryland and Virginia from their cruel task-masters
has not yet come, and may never come.* In the denial which I have
now made my motive is more a respectful consideration for the
opinions of the slave's friends than from my fear of being made an
accomplice in the general *conspiracy* against Slavery. I am ever
ready to write, speak, publish, organize, combine, and even to con-
spire against Slavery, when there is a reasonable hope of success.
Men who live by robbing their fellow-men of their labor and liberty,
have forfeited their right to know anything of the thoughts, feelings,
or purposes of those whom they rob and plunder. They have, by the
single act of slave-holding, voluntarily placed themselves beyond
the laws of justice and honor, and have become only fitted for com-
panionship with thieves and pirates—the common enemies of God
and of all mankind. While it shall be considered right to protect
one's self against thieves, burglars, robbers, and assassins, and to
slay a wild beast in the act of devouring his human prey, it can
never be wrong for the imbruted and whip-scarred slaves, or their
friends, to hunt, harass, and even strike down the traffickers in
human flesh. If anybody is disposed to think less of me on account
of this sentiment, or because I may have had a knowledge of what
was about to occur, and did not assume the base and detestable
character of an informer, he is a man whose good or bad opinion
of me may be equally repugnant and despicable. Entertaining this
sentiment, I may be asked why I did not join John Brown—the
noble old hero whose one right hand has shaken the foundation of
the American Union, and whose ghost will haunt the bed-chambers
of all the born and unborn slaveholders of Virginia through all
their generations, filling them with alarm and consternation! My
answer to this has already been given, at least impliedly given.

"The tools to those who can use them." Let every man work for the abolition of Slavery in his own way. I would help all and hinder none. My position in regard to the Harpers Ferry insurrection may be easily inferred from these remarks, and I shall be glad if those papers which have spoken of me in connection with it, would find room for this statement.

I have no apology for keeping out of the way of those gentlemanly United States Marshals, who are said to have paid Rochester a somewhat protracted visit lately with a view of an interview with me. A Government recognizing the validity of the Dred Scott decision, at such a time as this, is not likely to have any very charitable feelings towards me, and if I am to meet its representatives I prefer to do so at least upon equal terms. If I have committed any offense against society I have done so on the soil of the State of New York, and I should be perfectly willing *there* to be arraigned before an impartial jury; but I have quite insuperable objections to be caught in the hands of Mr. Buchanan, and *"bagged"* by Gov. Wise. For this appears to be the arrangement—Buchanan does the fighting and hunting, and Wise *"bags"* the game.

Some reflections may be made upon my leaving on a tour to England just at this time. I have only to say that my going to that country has been rather delayed than hastened by the insurrection at Harpers Ferry. All knew that I intended to leave here in the first week of November.

FREDERICK DOUGLASS.

9

Lincoln as Liberator[1]

Of the many instances in which Douglass spoke or wrote of Abraham Lincoln, the most notable was an address delivered on April 14, 1876, at the unveiling of a memorial monument depicting Lincoln and a slave whose shackles have been broken. The funds for the bronze statue had been raised by Negroes, and the exercises were honored by the presence of President Grant, his cabinet, and Supreme Court justices and Congressmen. Such an occasion called for Douglass as orator of the day. His speech, which Senator George S. Boutwell of Massachusetts termed the best of its kind "since the time of Mr. Webster," was a realistic appraisal of Lincoln's relationship to the Negro.

The sentiment that brings us here to-day is one of the noblest that can stir and thrill the human heart. It has crowned and made glorious the high places of all civilized nations with the grandest and most enduring works or art, designed to illustrate the characters and perpetuate the memories of great public men. It is the sentiment which from year to year adorns with fragrant and beautiful flowers the graves of our loyal, brave, and patriotic soldiers who fell in defence of the Union and liberty. It is the sentiment of gratitude and appreciation, which often, in the presence of many who hear me, has filled yonder heights of Arlington with the eloquence of eulogy and the sublime enthusiasm of poetry and song; a sentiment which can never die while the Republic lives.

For the first time in the history of our people, and in the history of the whole American people, we join in this high worship, and

[1] From *Oration Delivered on the Occasion of the Unveiling of the Freedmen's Monument in Memory of Abraham Lincoln, in Lincoln Park, Washington, D. C., April 14, 1876* (St. Louis, 1876), pp. 3–10, 14–15.

march conspicuously in the line of this time-honored custom. First things are always interesting, and this is one of our first things. It is the first time that, in this form and manner, we have sought to do honor to an American great man, however deserving and illustrious. I commend the fact to notice; let it be told in every part of the Republic; let men of all parties and opinions hear it; let those who despise us, not less than those who respect us, know that now and here, in the spirit of liberty, loyalty, and gratitude, let it be known everywhere, and by everybody who takes an interest in human progress and in the amelioration of the condition of mankind, that, in the presence and with the approval of the members of the American House of Representatives, reflecting the general sentiment of the country; that in the presence of that august body, the American Senate, representing the highest intelligence and the calmest judgment of the country; in the presence of the Supreme Court and Chief-Justice of the United States, to whose decisions we all patriotically bow; in the presence and under the steady eye of the honored and trusted President of the United States, with the members of his wise and patriotic Cabinet, we, the colored people, newly emancipated and rejoicing in our blood-bought freedom, near the close of the first century in the life of this Republic, have now and here unveiled, set apart, and dedicated a monument of enduring granite and bronze, in every line, feature, and figure of which the men of this generation may read, and those of after-coming generations may read, something of the exalted character and great works of Abraham Lincoln, the first martyr President of the United States.

Fellow-citizens, in what we have said and done today, and in what we may say and do hereafter, we disclaim everything like arrogance and assumption. We claim for ourselves no superior devotion to the character, history, and memory of the illustrious name whose monument we have here dedicated today. We fully comprehend the relation of Abraham Lincoln both to ourselves and to the white people of the United States. Truth is proper and beautiful at all times and in all places, and it is never more proper and beautiful in any case than when speaking of a great public man whose example is likely to be commended for honor and imitation long after his departure to the solemn shades, the silent continents of eternity. It must be admitted, truth compels me to admit, even here in the presence of the monument we have erected to his memory, Abraham Lincoln was not, in the fullest sense of the word, either our man or our model. In his interests, in his associations, in his habits of thought, and in his prejudices, he was a white man.

He was preëminently the white man's President, entirely devoted to the welfare of white men. He was ready and willing at any time during the first years of his administration to deny, postpone, and sacrifice the rights of humanity in the colored people to promote the welfare of the white people of this country. In all his education and feeling he was an American of the Americans. He came into the Presidential chair upon one principle alone, namely, opposition to the extension of slavery. His arguments in furtherance of this policy had their motive and mainspring in his patriotic devotion to the interests of his own race. To protect, defend, and perpetuate slavery in the states where it existed Abraham Lincoln was not less ready than any other President to draw the sword of the nation. He was ready to execute all the supposed guarantees of the United States Constitution in favor of the slave system anywhere inside the slave states. He was willing to pursue, recapture, and send back the fugitive slave to his master, and to suppress a slave rising for liberty, though his guilty master were already in arms against the Government. The race to which we belong were not the special objects of his consideration. Knowing this, I concede to you, my white fellow-citizens, a preëminence in this worship at once full and supreme. First, midst, and last, you and yours were the object of his deepest affection and his most earnest solicitude. You are the children of Abraham Lincoln. We are at best only his step-children; children by adoption, children by forces of circumstances and necessity. To you it especially belongs to sound his praises, to preserve and perpetuate his memory, to multiply his statues, to hang his pictures high upon your walls, and commend his example, for to you he was a great and glorious friend and benefactor. Instead of supplanting you at his altar, we would exhort you to build high his monuments; let them be of the most costly material, of the most cunning workmanship; let their forms be symmetrical, beautiful, and perfect; let their bases be upon solid rocks, and their summits lean against the unchanging blue, overhanging sky, and let them endure forever! But while in the abundance of your wealth, and in the fullness of your just and patriotic devotion, you do all this, we entreat you to despise not the humble offering we this day unveil to view; for while Abraham Lincoln saved for you a country, he delivered us from a bondage, according to Jefferson, one hour of which was worse than ages of the oppression your fathers rose in rebellion to oppose.

Fellow-citizens, ours is no new-born zeal and devotion—merely a thing of this moment. The name of Abraham Lincoln was near and dear to our hearts in the darkest and most perilous hours of the Republic. We were no more ashamed of him when shrouded in clouds of darkness, of doubt, and defeat than when we saw him crowned with victory, honor, and glory. Our faith in him was often taxed and strained to the uttermost, but it never failed. When he tarried long in the mountain; when he strangely told us that we were the cause of the war; when he still more strangely told us that we were to leave the land in which we were born; when he refused to employ our arms in defence of the Union; when, after accepting our services as colored soldiers, he refused to retaliate our murder and torture as colored prisoners; when he told us he would save the Union if he could with slavery; when he revoked the Proclamation of Emancipation of General Frémont; when he refused to remove the popular commander of the Army of the Potomac, in the days of its inaction and defeat, who was more zealous in his efforts to protect slavery than to suppress rebellion; when we saw all this, and more, we were at times grieved, stunned, and greatly bewildered; but our hearts believed while they ached and bled. Nor was this, even at that time, a blind and unreasoning superstition. Despite the mist and haze that surrounded him; despite the tumult, the hurry, and confusion of the hour, we were able to take a comprehensive view of Abraham Lincoln, and to make reasonable allowance for the circumstances of his position. We saw him, measured him, and estimated him; not by stray utterances to injudicious and tedious delegations, who often tried his patience; not by isolated facts torn from their connection; not by any partial and imperfect glimpses, caught at inopportune moments; but by a broad survey, in the light of the stern logic of great events, and in view of that divinity which shapes our ends, rough hew them how we will, we

came to the conclusion that the hour and the man of our redemp-
tion had somehow met in the person of Abraham Lincoln. It mattered little to us what language he might employ on special occasions; it mattered little to us, when we fully knew him, whether
he was swift or slow in his movements; it was enough for us that
Abraham Lincoln was at the head of a great movement, and was
in living and earnest sympathy with that movement, which, in the
nature of things, must go on until slavery should be utterly and
forever abolished in the United States.

When, therefore, it shall be asked what we have to do with the
memory of Abraham Lincoln, or what Abraham Lincoln had to
do with us, the answer is ready, full, and complete. Though he loved
Cæsar less than Rome, though the Union was more to him than
our freedom or our future, under his wise and beneficent rule we
saw ourselves gradually lifted from the depths of slavery to the
heights of liberty and manhood; under his wise and beneficent rule,
and by measures approved and vigorously pressed by him, we saw
that the handwriting of ages, in the form of prejudice and proscription, was rapidly fading away from the face of our whole country;
under his rule, and in due time, about as soon after all as the country could tolerate the strange spectacle, we saw our brave sons and
brothers laying off the rags of bondage, and being clothed all over
in the blue uniforms of the soldiers of the United States; under his
rule we saw two hundred thousand of our dark and dusky people
responding to the call of Abraham Lincoln, and with muskets on
their shoulders, and eagles on their buttons, timing their high foot-
steps to liberty and union under the national flag; under his rule
we saw the independence of the black republic of Haiti, the special
object of slaveholding aversion and horror, fully recognized, and her
minister, a colored gentleman, duly received here in the city of
Washington; under his rule we saw the internal slave-trade, which
so long disgraced the nation, abolished, and slavery abolished in
the District of Columbia; under his rule we saw for the first time
the law enforced against the foreign slave trade, and the first slave-
trader hanged like any other pirate or murderer; under his rule,
assisted by the greatest captain of our age, and his inspiration, we
saw the Confederate States, based upon the idea that our race must
be slaves, and slave forever, battered to pieces and scattered to the

four winds; under his rule, and in the fullness of time, we saw Abraham Lincoln, after giving the slaveholders three months' grace in which to save their hateful slave system, penning the immortal paper, which, though special in its language, was general in its principles and effect, making slavery forever impossible in the United States. Though we waited long, we saw all this and more.

Can any colored man, or any white man friendly to the freedom of all men, ever forget the night which followed the first day of January, 1863, when the world was to see if Abraham Lincoln would prove to be as good as his word? I shall never forget that memorable night, when in a distant city I waited and watched at a public meeting, with three thousand others not less anxious than myself, for the word of deliverance which we have heard read today. Nor shall I ever forget the outburst of joy and thanksgiving that rent the air when the lightning brought to us the Emancipation Proclamation. In that happy hour we forgot all delay, and forgot all tardiness, forgot that the President had bribed the rebels to lay down their arms by a promise to withhold the bolt which would smite the slave-system with destruction; and we were thenceforward willing to allow the President all the latitude of time, phraseology, and every honorable device that statesmanship might require for the achievement of a great and beneficent measure of liberty and progress.

Fellow-citizens, there is little necessity on this occasion to speak at length and critically of this great and good man, and of his high mission in the world. That ground has been fully occupied and completely covered both here and elsewhere. The whole field of fact and fancy has been gleaned and garnered. Any man can say things that are true of Abraham Lincoln, but no man can say anything that is new of Abraham Lincoln. His personal traits and public acts are better known to the American people than are those of any other man of his age. He was a mystery to no man who saw him and heard him. Though high in position, the humblest could approach him and feel at home in his presence. Though deep, he was transparent; though strong, he was gentle; though decided and pronounced in his convictions, he was tolerant towards those who differed from him, and patient under reproaches. Even those who only knew him through his public utterance obtained a tolerably clear idea of his character and personality. The image of the man went out with his words, and those who read them knew him.

I have said that President Lincoln was a white man, and shared the prejudices common to his countrymen towards the colored race. Looking back to his times and to the condition of his country, we are compelled to admit that this unfriendly feeling on his part may be safely set down as one element of his wonderful success in organizing the loyal American people for the tremendous conflict before them, and bringing them safely through that conflict. His great mission was to accomplish two things: first, to save his country from dismemberment and ruin; and, second, to free his country from the great crime of slavery. To do one or the other, or both, he must have the earnest sympathy and the powerful coöperation of his loyal fellow-countrymen. Without this primary and essential condition to success his efforts must have been vain and utterly fruitless. Had he put the abolition of slavery before the salvation of the Union, he would have inevitably driven from him a powerful class of the American people and rendered resistance to rebellion impossible. Viewed from the genuine abolition ground, Mr. Lincoln seemed tardy, cold, dull, and indifferent; but measuring him by the sentiment of his country, a sentiment he was bound as a statesman to consult, he was swift, zealous, radical, and determined. . . .

Fellow-citizens, the fourteenth day of April, 1865, of which this is the eleventh anniversary, is now and will ever remain a memorable day in the annals of this Republic. It was on the evening of this day, while a fierce and sanguinary rebellion was in the last stages of its desolating power; while its armies were broken and scattered before the invincible armies of Grant and Sherman; while a great nation, torn and rent by war, was already beginning to raise to the skies loud anthems of joy at the dawn of peace, it was startled, amazed, and overwhelmed by the crowning crime of slavery—the assassination of Abraham Lincoln. It was a new crime, a pure act of malice. No purpose of the rebellion was to be served by it. It was the simple gratification of a hell-black spirit of revenge. But it has done good after all. It has filled the country with a deeper abhorrence of slavery and a deeper love for the great liberator. . . .

Had Abraham Lincoln died from any of the numerous ills to which flesh is heir; had he reached that good old age of which his vigorous constitution and his temperate habits gave promise; had he been permitted to see the end of his great work; had the solemn curtain of death come down but gradually—we should still have been smitten with a heavy grief, and treasured his name lovingly. But dying as he did die, by the red hand of violence, killed, assassinated, taken off without warning, not because of personal hate—for no man who knew Abraham Lincoln could hate him—but because of his fidelity to union and liberty, he is doubly dear to us, and his memory will be precious forever.

Fellow-citizens, I end, as I began, with congratulations. We have done a good work for our race today. In doing honor to the memory of our friend and liberator, we have been doing highest honors to ourselves and those who come after us; we have been fastening ourselves to a name and fame imperishable and immortal; we have also been defending ourselves from a blighting scandal. When now it shall be said that the colored man is soulless, that he has no appreciation of benefits or benefactors; when the foul reproach of ingratitude is hurled at us, and it is attempted to scourge us beyond the range of human brotherhood, we may calmly point to the monument we have this day erected to the memory of Abraham Lincoln.

10

The High Wall of Race[1]

To an essay, "The Color Line," written in 1881, Douglass brought the full complement of his powers in reasoning and exposition. One of his most penetrating pieces, it foreshadows the trenchant observation made by W. E. B. Du-Bois 20 years later: "The problem of the twentieth century is the problem of the color-line."

THE COLOR LINE

Few evils are less accessible to the force of reason, or more tenacious of life and power, than a long-standing prejudice. It is a moral disorder, which creates the conditions necessary to its own existence, and fortifies itself by refusing all contradiction. It paints a hateful picture according to its own diseased imagination, and distorts the features of the fancied original to suit the portrait. As those who believe in the visibility of ghosts can easily see them, so it is always easy to see repulsive qualities in those we despise and hate.

Prejudice of race has at some time in their history afflicted all nations. "I am more holy than thou" is the boast of races, as well as that of the Pharisee. Long after the Norman invasion and the decline of Norman power, long after the sturdy Saxon had shaken off the dust of his humiliation and was grandly asserting his great qualities in all directions, the descendants of the invaders continued to regard their Saxon brothers as made of coarser clay than themselves, and were not well pleased when one of the former subject race came between the sun and their nobility. Having seen the Saxon a menial, a hostler, and a common drudge, oppressed and

[1] From *The North American Review*, 132 (July, 1881).

dejected for centuries, it was easy to invest him with all sorts of odious peculiarities, and to deny him all manly predicates. Though eight hundred years have passed away since Norman power entered England, and the Saxon has for centuries been giving his learning, his literature, his language, and his laws to the world more successfully than any other people on the globe, men in that country still boast their Norman origin and Norman perfections. This superstition of former greatness serves to fill out the shriveled sides of a meaningless race-pride which holds over after its power has vanished. With a very different lesson from the one this paper is designed to impress, the great Daniel Webster once told the people of Massachusetts (whose prejudices in the particular instance referred to were right) that they "had conquered the sea, and had conquered the land," but that "it remained for them to conquer their prejudices." At one time we are told that the people in some of the towns of Yorkshire cherished a prejudice so strong and violent against strangers and foreigners that one who ventured to pass through their streets would be pelted with stones.

Of all the races and varieties of men which have suffered from this feeling, the colored people of this country have endured most. They can resort to no disguises which will enable them to escape its deadly aim. They carry in front the evidence which marks them for persecution. They stand at the extreme point of difference from the Caucasian race, and their African origin can be instantly recognized, though they may be several removes from the typical African race. They may remonstrate like Shylock—"Hath not a Jew eyes? hath not a Jew hands, organs, dimensions, senses, affections, passions? fed with the same food, hurt with the same weapons, subject to the same diseases, healed by the same means, warmed and cooled by the same summer and winter, as a Christian is?"— but such eloquence is unavailing. They are Negroes—and that is enough, in the eye of this unreasoning prejudice, to justify indignity and violence. In nearly every department of American life they are confronted by this insidious influence. It fills the air. It meets them at the workshop and factory, when they apply for work. It meets them at the church, at the hotel, at the ballot-box, and worst of all, it meets them in the jury-box. Without crime or offense against law or gospel, the colored man is the Jean Valjean of American society. He has escaped from the galleys, and hence all presumptions are against him. The workshop denies him work, and the inn denies him shelter; the ballot-box a fair vote, and the jury-box a fair trial. He has ceased to be the slave of an individual, but has in some sense become the slave of society. He may not now be bought and sold like a beast in the market, but he is the trammeled victim of a prejudice, well calculated to repress his manly ambition, paralyze his energies, and make him a dejected and spiritless man, if not a sullen enemy to society, fit to prey upon life and property and to make trouble generally.

When this evil spirit is judge, jury, and prosecutor, nothing less than overwhelming evidence is sufficient to overcome the force of unfavorable presumptions.

Everything against the person with the hated color is promptly taken for granted; while everything in his favor is received with suspicion and doubt.

A boy of this color is found in his bed tied, mutilated, and bleeding, when forthwith all ordinary experience is set aside, and he is presumed to have been guilty of the outrage upon himself; weeks and months he is kept on trial for the offense, and every effort is made to entangle the poor fellow in the confused meshes of expert testimony (the least trustworthy of all evidence). This same spirit, which promptly assumes everything against us, just as readily denies or explains away everything in our favor. We are not, as a race, even permitted to appropriate the virtues and achievements of our individual representatives. Manliness, capacity, learning, laudable ambition, heroic service, by any of our number, are easily placed to the credit of the superior race. One drop of Teutonic blood is enough to account for all good and great qualities occasionally coupled with a colored skin; and on the other hand, one drop of Negro blood, though in the veins of a man of Teutonic whiteness, is enough of which to predicate all offensive and ignoble qualities. In presence of this spirit, if a crime is committed, and the criminal is not positively known, a suspicious-looking colored man is sure to have been seen in the neighborhood. If an unarmed colored man is shot down and dies in his tracks, a jury, under the influence of this spirit, does not hesitate to find the murdered man the real criminal, and the murderer innocent.

Now let us examine this subject a little more closely. It is claimed that this wonder-working prejudice—this moral magic that can change virtue into vice, and innocence to crime; which makes the dead man the murderer, and holds the living homicide harmless—is a natural, instinctive, and invincible attribute of the white race, and one that cannot be eradicated; that even evolution itself cannot carry us beyond or above it. Alas for this poor suffering world (for four-fifths of mankind are colored), if this claim be true! In that case men are forever doomed to injustice, oppression, hate, and strife; and the religious sentiment of the world, with its grand idea of human brotherhood, its "peace on earth and good-will to men," and its golden rule, must be voted a dream, a delusion, and a snare.

But is this color prejudice the natural and inevitable thing it claims to be? If it is so, then it is utterly idle to write against it, preach, pray, or legislate against it, or pass constitutional amendments against it. Nature will have her course, and one might as well preach and pray to a horse against running, to a fish against swimming, or to a bird against flying. Fortunately, however, there is good ground for calling in question this high pretension of a vulgar and wicked prepossession.

If I could talk with all my white fellow-countrymen on this subject, I would say to them, in the language of Scripture: "Come and let us reason together." Now, without being too elementary and formal, it may be stated here that there are at least seven points which candid men will be likely to admit, but which, if admitted, will prove fatal to the popular thought and practice of the times.

First. If what we call prejudice against color be natural, i.e., a part of human nature itself, it follows that it must be co-extensive with human nature, and will and must manifest itself whenever and wherever the two races are brought into contact. It would not vary with either latitude, longitude, or altitude; but like fire and gunpowder, whenever brought together, there would be an explosion of contempt, aversion, and hatred.

Secondly. If it can be shown that there is anywhere on the globe any considerable country where the contact of the African and the Caucasian is not distinguished by this explosion of race-wrath, there is reason to doubt that the prejudice is an ineradicable part of human nature.

Thirdly. If this so-called natural, instinctive prejudice can be satisfactorily accounted for by facts and considerations wholly apart from the color features of the respective races, thus placing it among the things subject to human volition and control, we may venture to deny the claim set up for it in the name of human nature.

Fourthly. If any considerable number of white people have overcome this prejudice in themselves, have cast it out as an unworthy sentiment, and have survived the operation, the fact shows that this prejudice is not at any rate a vital part of human nature, and may be eliminated from the race without harm.

Fifthly. If this prejudice shall, after all, prove to be, in its essence and in its natural manifestation, simply a prejudice against condition, and not against race or color, and that it disappears when this or that condition is absent, then the argument drawn from the nature of the Caucasian race falls to the ground.

Sixthly. If prejudice of race and color is only natural in the sense that ignorance, superstition, bigotry, and vice are natural, then it has no better defense than they, and should be despised and put away from human relations as an enemy to the peace, good order, and happiness of human society.

Seventhly. If, still further, this aversion to the Negro arises out of the fact that he is as we see him, poor, spiritless, ignorant, and degraded, then whatever is humane, noble, and superior, in the mind of the superior and more fortunate race, will desire that all arbitrary barriers against his manhood, intelligence, and elevation shall be removed, and a fair chance in the race of life be given him.

The first of these propositions does not require discussion. It commends itself to the understanding at once. Natural qualities are common and universal, and do not change essentially on the mountain or in the valley. I come therefore to the second point—the existence of countries where this malignant prejudice, as we know it in America, does not prevail; where character, not color, is the passport to consideration; where the right of the black man to be a man, and a man among men, is not questioned; where he may, without offense, even presume to be a gentleman. That there are such countries in the world there is ample evidence. Intelligent and observing travelers, having no theory to support, men whose testimony would be received without question in respect of any other matter, and should not be questioned in this, tell us that they find no color prejudice in Europe, except among Americans who reside there. In England and on the Continent, the colored man is no more an object of hate than any other person. He mingles with the multitude unquestioned, without offense given or received. During the two years which the writer spent abroad, though he was much in society, and was sometimes in the company of lords and ladies, he does not remember one word, look, or gesture that indicated the slightest aversion to him on account of color. His experience was not in this respect exceptional or singular. Messrs. Remond, Ward, Garnet, Brown, Pennington, Crummell, and Bruce, all of them colored, and some of them black, bear the same testimony. If what these gentlemen say (and it can be corroborated by a thousand witnesses) is true there is no prejudice against color in England, save as it is carried there by Americans—carried there as a moral disease from an infected country. It is American, not European; local, not general; limited, not universal, and must be ascribed to artificial conditions, and not to any fixed and universal law of nature.

The third point is: Can this prejudice against color, as it is called, be accounted for by circumstances outside and independent of race or color? If it can be thus explained, an incubus may be removed from the breasts of both the white and the black people of this country, as well as from that large intermediate population which has sprung up between these alleged irreconcilable extremes. It will help us to see that it is not necessary that the Ethiopian shall change his skin, nor needful that the white man shall change the essential elements of his nature, in order that mutual respect and consideration may exist between the two races.

Now it is easy to explain the conditions outside of race or color from which may spring feelings akin to those which we call prejudice. A man without the ability or the disposition to pay a just debt does not feel at ease in the presence of his creditor. He does not want to meet him on the street, or in the market-place. Such meeting makes him uncomfortable. He would rather find fault with the bill than pay the debt, and the creditor himself will soon develop in the eyes of the debtor qualities not altogether to his taste.

Someone has well said, we may easily forgive those who injure us, but it is hard to forgive those whom we injure. The greatest injury this side of death, which one human being can inflict on another, is to enslave him, to blot out his personality, degrade his manhood, and sink him to the condition of a beast of burden; and just this has been done here during more than two centuries. No other people under heaven, of whatever type or endowments, could have been so enslaved without falling into contempt and scorn on the part of those enslaving them. Their slavery would itself stamp them with odious features, and give their oppressors arguments in favor of oppression. Besides the long years of wrong and injury inflicted upon the colored race in this country, and the effect of these wrongs upon that race, morally, intellectually, and physically, corrupting their morals, darkening their minds, and twisting their bodies and limbs out of all approach to symmetry, there has been a mountain of gold—uncounted millions of dollars—resting upon them with crushing weight. During all the years of their bondage, the slave master had a direct interest in discrediting the personality of those he held as property. Every man who had a thousand dollars so invested had a thousand reasons for painting the black man as fit only for slavery. Having made him the companion of horses and mules, he naturally sought to justify himself by assuming that the Negro was not much better than a mule. The holders of twenty hundred million dollars' worth of property in human chattels procured the means of influencing press, pulpit, and politician, and through these instrumentalities they belittled our virtues and magnified our vices, and have made us odious in the eyes of the world. Slavery had the power at one time to make and unmake Presidents, to construe the law, dictate the policy, set the fashion in national manners and customs, interpret the Bible, and control the church; and, naturally enough, the old masters set themselves up as much too high as they set the manhood of the Negro too low. Out of the depths of slavery has come this prejudice and this color line. It is broad enough and black enough to explain all the malign influences which assail the newly emancipated millions today. In reply to this argument it will perhaps be said that the Negro has no slavery now to contend with, and that having been free during the last sixteen years, he ought by this time to have contradicted the degrading qualities which slavery formerly ascribed to him. All very true as to the letter, but utterly false as to the spirit. Slavery is indeed gone, but its shadow still lingers over the country and poisons more or less the moral atmosphere of all sections of the republic. The money motive for assailing the Negro which slavery represented is indeed absent, but love of power and dominion, strengthened by two centuries of irresponsible power, still remains.

Having now shown how slavery created and sustained this prejudice against race and color, and the powerful motive for its creation, the other four points made against it need not be discussed in detail and at length, but may only be referred to in a general way.

If what is called the instinctive aversion of the white race for the colored, when analyzed, is seen to be the same as that which men feel or have felt toward other objects wholly apart from color; if it should be the same as that sometimes exhibited by the haughty and rich to the humble and poor, the same as the Brahmin feels toward the lower caste, the same as the Norman felt toward the Saxon, the same as that cherished by the Turk against Christians, the same as Christians have felt toward the Jews, the same as that which murders a Christian in Wallachia, calls him a "dog" in Constantinople, oppresses and persecutes a Jew in Berlin, hunts down a socialist in St. Petersburg, drives a Hebrew from an hotel at Saratoga, that scorns the Irishman in London, the same as Catholics once felt for Protestants, the same as that which insults, abuses, and kills the Chinaman on the Pacific slope—then may we well enough affirm that this prejudice really has nothing whatever to do with race or color, and that it has its motive and mainspring in some other source with which the mere facts of color and race have nothing to do.

After all, some very well informed and very well meaning people will read what I have now said, and what seems to me so just and reasonable, and will still insist that the color of the Negro has something to do with the feeling entertained toward him; that the white man naturally shudders at the thought of contact with one who is black—that the impulse is one which he can neither resist nor control. Let us see if this conclusion is a sound one. An argument is unsound when it proves too little or too much, or when it proves nothing. If color is an offense, it is so, entirely apart from the man-hood it envelops. There must be something in color of itself to kindle rage and inflame hate, and render the white man generally uncomfortable. If the white man were really so constituted that color were, in itself, a torment to him, this grand old earth of ours would be no place for him. Colored objects confront him here at every point of the compass. If he should shrink and shudder every time he sees anything dark, he would have little time for anything else. He would require a colorless world to live in—a world where flowers, fields, and floods should all be of snowy whiteness; where rivers, lakes, and oceans should all be white; where islands, capes, and continents should all be white; where all the men, and women, and children should be white; where all the fish of the sea, all the birds of the air, all the "cattle upon a thousand hills," should be white; where the heavens above and the earth beneath should be white, and where day and night should not be divided by light and darkness, but the world should be one eternal scene of light. In such a white world, the entrance of a black man would be hailed with joy by the inhabitants. Anybody or anything would be welcome that would break the oppressive and tormenting monotony of the all-prevailing white.

In the abstract, there is no prejudice against color. No man shrinks from another because he is clothed in a suit of black, nor offended with his boots because they are black. We are told by those who have resided there that a white man in Africa comes to think that ebony is about the proper color for man. Good old Thomas Whitson—a noble old Quaker—a man of rather odd appearance—used to say that even he would be handsome if he could change public opinion.

Aside from the curious contrast to himself, the white child feels nothing on the first sight of a colored man. Curiosity is the only feeling. The office of color in the color line is a very plain and sub-ordinate one. It simply advertises the objects of oppression, insult, and persecution. It is not the maddening liquor, but the black letters on the sign telling the world where it may be had. It is not the hated Quaker, but the broad brim and the plain coat. It is not the hateful Cain, but the mark by which he is known. The color is innocent enough, but things with which it is coupled make it hated.

Slavery, ignorance, stupidity, servility, poverty, dependence are undesirable conditions. When these shall cease to be coupled with color, there will be no color line drawn. It may help in this direction to observe a few of the inconsistencies of the color-line feeling, for it is neither uniform in its operations nor consistent in its principles. Its contradictions in the latter respect would be amusing if the feeling itself were not so deserving of unqualified abhorrence. Our Californian brothers, of Hibernian descent, hate the Chinaman, and kill him, and when asked why they do so, their answer is that a Chinaman is so industrious he will do all the work, and can live by wages upon which other people would starve. When the same people and others are asked why they hate the colored people, the answer is that they are indolent and wasteful, and cannot take care of themselves. Statesmen of the South will tell you that the Negro is too ignorant and stupid properly to exercise the elective franchise, and yet his greatest offense is that he acts with the only party intelligent enough in the eyes of the nation to legislate for the country. In one breath they tell us that the Negro is so weak in intellect, and so destitute of manhood, that he is but the echo of designing white men, and yet in another they will virtually tell you that the Negro is so clear in his moral perceptions, so firm in purpose, so steadfast in his convictions, that he cannot be persuaded by arguments or intimidated by threats, and that nothing but the shot-gun can restrain him from voting for the men and measures he approves. They shrink back in horror from contact with the Negro as a man and a gentleman, but like him very well as a barber, waiter, coachman, or cook. As a slave, he could ride anywhere, side by side with his white master, but as a freeman, he must be thrust into the smoking-car. As a slave, he could go into the first cabin; as a freeman, he was not allowed abaft the wheel. Formerly it was said he was incapable of learning, and at the same time it was a crime against the state for any man to teach him to read. Today he is said to be originally and permanently inferior to the white race, and yet wild apprehensions are expressed lest six millions of this inferior race will somehow or other manage to rule over thirty-five millions of the superior race. If inconsistency can prove the hollowness of anything, certainly the emptiness of this pretense that color has any terrors is easily shown. The trouble is that most men, and especially mean men, want to have something under them. The rich man would have the poor man, the white would have the black, the Irish would have the Negro, and the Negro must have a dog, if he can get nothing higher in the scale of intelligence to dominate. This feeling is one of the vanities which enlightenment will dispel. A good but simple-minded Abolitionist said to me that he was not ashamed to walk with me down Broadway arm-in-arm, in open daylight, and evidently thought he was saying something that must be very pleasing to my self-importance, but it occurred to me, at the moment, this man does not dream of any reason why I might be ashamed to walk arm-in-arm with him through Broadway in open daylight. Riding in a stage-coach from Concord, New Hampshire, to Vergennes, Vermont, many years ago, I found myself on very pleasant terms with all the passengers through the night, but the morning light came to me as it comes to the stars; I was as Dr. Beecher says he was at the first fire he witnessed, when a bucket of cold water was poured down his back—"the fire was not put out, but he was." The fact is, the higher the colored man rises in the scale of society, the less prejudice does he meet.

The writer has met and mingled freely with the leading great men of his time,—at home and abroad, in public halls and private houses, on the platform and at the fireside,—and can remember no instance when among such men has he been made to feel himself an object of aversion. Men who are really great are too great to be small. This was gloriously true of the late Abraham Lincoln, William H. Seward, Salmon P. Chase, Henry Wilson, John P. Hale, Lewis Tappan, Edmund Quincy, Joshua R. Giddings, Gerrit Smith, and Charles Sumner, and many others among the dead. Good taste will not permit me now to speak of the living, except to say that the number of those who rise superior to prejudice is great and increasing. Let those who wish to see what is to be the future of America, as relates to races and race relations, attend, as I have attended, during the administration of President Hayes, the grand diplomatic receptions at the executive mansion, and see there, as I have seen, in its splendid east room the wealth, culture, refinement, and beauty of the nation assembled, and with it the eminent representatives of other nations,—the swarthy Turk with his "fez," the Englishman shining with gold, the German, the Frenchman, the

Spaniard, the Japanese, the Chinaman, the Caucasian, the Mongolian, the Sandwich Islander, and the Negro,—all moving about freely, each respecting the rights and dignity of the other, and neither receiving nor giving offense.

"Then let us pray that come it may,
As come it will for a' that,
That sense and worth, o'er a' the earth,
May bear the gree, and a' that;

"That man to man, the world o'er,
Shall brothers be, for a' that."

11

Defender at the Bar[1]

After the Civil War many of Douglass's speeches to white audiences were devoted to the condition of the Negro— his past, present, and prospects. Typical of such an address was the one which he delivered at the annual meeting of the American Missionary Association, held at Lowell, Massachusetts, late in 1894. The last major address by the seventy-seven-year-old Douglass, its title, "A Defence of the Negro Race," might have epitomized his long career.

I esteem it an honor to have been invited to speak a word in this presence upon this very interesting occasion. I am here, however, not so much to deliver an address, or to make a speech, as to put myself on record. I am here to pay a debt long due. I have wished, by my presence here, to emphasize my gratitude to the members and friends of this Association for the beneficent work which they have done, and which they are still doing, for the people with whom I am identified. I would not disparage the labors of any other organization in this direction inside of the church. I am thankful to all such, but I know of none to which the colored people of the Southern States are more indebted for effective service than to this American Missionary Association.

Long before the abolition of slavery, this organization bore a consistent and faithful testimony against that stupendous wrong. When it was abolished this Association did not disband nor discontinue its work, but went forward as earnestly as ever to advance, enlighten and elevate the colored people of the South.

It saw very clearly the evils inherited from the slave's former con-

[1] From *Address by Hon. Frederick Douglass at the Annual Meeting of the American Missionary Association, in Lowell, Mass., 1894* (New York: American Missionary Association Bible House, 1894), pp. 1–3, 5–6, 8.

dition, and heroically wrought to remove those evils. It had the good fortune to take the tide at its flood, and it seized the opportunity with skill and effect. The sword of the nation had not returned to its scabbard, the smoke had not rolled away from the battlefield, when its noble and efficient missionaries, in the face of popular indifference at the North, and the manifest hostility of the old master class at the South, bravely lighted and held aloft the torch of education, and carried morals, religion, truth and training to the darkest sections of that country.

I have seen some of those missionaries, and have been compelled to admire them. Many of them educated and refined, accustomed to all the elegances that wealth and position could command, they did not hesitate to leave their comfortable homes and face Southern scorn, ostracism and persecution in order to lift up and enlighten the despised freedman.

This spectacle was grand and inspiring; with a zeal that never grew cold, a courage that never quailed, a faith that never wavered, they dared to take their stand by the side of the Negro in all the storms incident to his early emancipation.

When invited by your esteemed secretary to be present on this occasion, although I have not heretofore attended these annual meetings, and am conscious of no special fitness for speaking upon such occasions, I still felt that I was so identified with the cause of the oppressed, that I could not do less than publicly to acknowledge, in their name and in my own, our common indebtedness to this Association for its successful efforts in our behalf. It would be easy to show by the facts of the history of this Association that the colored people of the South owe their success in shaking off the moral darkness and ignorance, inherited from long years of slavery, in large measure to this Association.

It has sometimes been thought and said that Northern benevolence has already done enough for the moral and religious improvement of the Negro, and that the time has arrived when such help is no longer needed, that the Negro should now be left to take care of himself, that the duty of the white people of the country was fully and fairly performed when they restored the Negro to his freedom.

In answer to this position, I have to say that the claims of the Negro, viewed in the light of justice and fair play, are not so easily satisfied. The simple act of emancipation was indeed a great and glorious one, but it did not remove the consequences of slavery, nor could it atone for the centuries of wrong endured by the liberated bondman. It was a great and glorious thing to put an end to his physical bondage, but there was left to him a dreadful legacy of moral and intellectual deformity, which the abolition of physical bondage could not remove. It might well be said of him, as is said in the scriptures, "the whole head is sick, and the whole heart faint. From the sole of the foot even unto the head, there is no soundness in it but wounds and bruises and putrifying sores; They have not been closed, neither bound up, neither mollified with ointment."

In answer to the question as to what shall be done with the Negro, I have sometimes replied, "Do nothing with him, give him fair play and let him alone." But in reporting me, it has been found convenient and agreeable to place the emphasis of my speech on one part of my sentence. They willingly accepted my idea of letting the Negro alone, but not so my idea of giving the Negro fair play. It has always been easier for some of the American people to imitate the priest and the Levite, rather than the example of the good Samaritan; to let the Negro alone rather than to give him fair play. Even here in New England—the most enlightened and benevolent section of our country—the Negro has been excluded from nearly all profitable employments. I speak from experience. I came here from the South fifty-six years ago, with a good trade in my hands, and might have commanded by my trade three dollars a day, but my white brethren, while praying for their daily bread, were not willing that I should obtain mine by the same means open to them. I was compelled to work for one dollar a day, when others working at my trade were receiving three dollars a day.

But to return. When we consider the long years of slavery, the years of enforced ignorance, the years of injustice, of cruel strifes and degradation to which the Negro was doomed, the duty of the nation is not, and cannot be, performed by simply letting him alone.

If Northern benevolence could send a missionary to every dark corner of the South, if it could place a church on every hilltop in the South, a schoolhouse in every valley, and support a preacher in the one, and a teacher in the other, for fifty years to come, they could not then even compensate the poor freedman for the long years of wrong and suffering he has been compelled to endure. The people of the North should remember that slavery and the degradation of the Negro were inflicted by the power of the nation, that the North was a consenting party to the wrong, and that a common sin can only be atoned and condoned by a common repentance. . . .

Under the whole heavens, there never was a people emancipated under conditions more unfavorable to mental, moral and physical improvement than were the slaves of our Southern States. They were emancipated not by the moral judgment of the nation as a whole; they were emancipated not as a blessing to themselves, but as a punishment to their masters; not to strengthen the emancipated, but to weaken the rebels, and, naturally enough, taking the emancipation in this sense, the old master class have resented it and have resolved to make his freedom a curse rather than a blessing to the Negro. In many instances they have been quite successful in accomplishing this purpose. Then the manner of emancipation was against the Negro. He was turned loose to the open sky without a foot of earth on which to stand; without a single farming implement; he was turned loose to the elements, to hunger, to destitution; without money, without friends; and to endure the pitiless storm of the old master's wrath. The old master had in his possession the land and the power to crush the Negro, and the Negro in return had no power of defence. The difference between his past condition and his present condition is that in the past the old master class could say to him, "You shall work for me or I will whip you to death"; in the present condition he can say to him, "You shall work for me or I will starve you to death." And to-day the Negro is in this latter condition.

No other nation ever treated a liberated people in such wise. When Russia emancipated her slaves to the number of twenty millions, she gave the head of each family three acres of ground, and implements with which to till the soil; that emancipation was merciful to the serf and honorable to a despotic government. It is to be regretted that no such honor is to be accorded to this nation and government in its treatment of its emancipated slaves. They were turned loose, sick and well; strong and weak; young and old; in a state of utter destitution, hardly owning the clothes on their backs. . . .

When we consider the destitution in which the colored people

of the United States were when emancipated, the wonder is not that
they are so far in the rear of the white man's civilization, but that
their advancement has been as rapid and complete as the evidence
demonstrates. Beginning with nothing, they are now able to say that
they pay taxes in the State of Georgia on eight millions; in Louisiana on twenty millions, and in other States accumulated wealth in
proportion; while in point of intellectual improvement their progress, according to the statistics of this Association, considering all the
circumstances, has not only been creditable, but amazing. A little
more than thirty years ago there was not a colored newspaper published in all the Southern States. There are now hundreds. We have
now scores of educated ministers, thousands of teachers, hundreds
of lawyers, and any number of doctors, where before our race was on
a dead level of illiteracy and ignorance.

Just now our Southern brethren are inviting the sympathy of their
fellow citizens on the ground that they are struggling with a terrible
Negro problem, and one which has given them a very large measure
of trouble. In the first place, I object to the origin of the title given
to this problem. I hold that it is a misnomer and misleading. It is a
crafty appeal to the popular prejudice entertained against the
Negro. It is the cunning that gives a dog a bad name in order to
have him hanged. I deny that they have anything on their hands at
the South which can be properly called a Negro problem. The trouble there is not with the Negro, but with his white oppressors. It
can be more properly called a white than a black problem, since its
solution depends more upon the action of white men than upon
that of black men. It is, however, not a white man's problem nor a
black man's problem, but a great national problem which involves
the honor or dishonor, the glory or the shame, of the whole American people, and is within their power to solve in one way or the
other. . . .

With all the discouraging circumstances that now surround what
is improperly called the Negro problem, I do not despair of a better
day. It is sometimes said that the condition of the colored man
to-day is worse than it was in the time of slavery. To me this is simply an extravagance. We now have the organic law of the land on
our side. We have thousands of teachers, and hundreds of thousands
of pupils attending schools; we can now count our friends by the

million. In many of the States we have the elective franchise; in some of them we have colored office-holders. It is no small advantage that we are citizens of this Republic by special amendment of the Constitution. The very resistance that we now meet on Southern railroads, steamboats and hotels is evidence of our progress. It is not the Negro in his degradation that is objected to, but the Negro educated, cultivated and refined. The Negro who fails to respect himself, who makes no provision for himself or his family, and is content to live the life of a vagabond, meets no resistance. He is just where he is desired by his enemies. Perhaps you will say that this proves that education, wealth and refinement will do nothing for the Negro; but the answer to this is, "that the hair of the dog will cure the bite" eventually. All people suddenly springing from a lowly condition have to pass through a period of probation. At first they are denounced as "upstarts," but the "upstarts" of one generation are the élite of the next.

The history of the great Anglo-Saxon race should encourage the Negro to hope on and hope ever, and work on and work ever. They were once the slaves of the Normans; they were despised and insulted. They were looked upon as of coarser clay than the haughty Norman. Their language was despised and repudiated, but where to-day is the haughty Norman? What people and what language now rock the world by their power?

My hope for the Negro is largely based upon his enduring qualities. No persecutions, no proscriptions, no hardships are able to extinguish him. He neither dies out, nor goes out. He is here to stay, and while here he will partake of the blessings of your education, your progress, your civilization, and your Christian religion. His appeal to you to-day is for an equal chance in the race of life, and, dark and stormy as the present appears, his appeal will not go unanswered.

PART TWO

THE WORLD LOOKS AT DOUGLASS

12

"Magnificent Orator"

*Frederick Douglass ranked high as a public speaker
in an age when oratory was in flower. The anti-slavery rostrum
had given him his schooling in public address, as it had to
many others. It was his genius as an orator that won him his
fame in his day and upon which much of his historical reputation rests. His contemporaries left innumerable references to
his abilities as a speaker, of which the following quartette is
representative. The first, by N. P. Rogers, editor of the* Herald
of Freedom, *published at Concord, New Hampshire, was written four scant months after Douglass had joined the abolitionists; the second is by William G. Allen, professor of rhetoric
and belles lettres at Central College in McGrawville, New
York, in 1852. The final estimates are by Thomas Wentworth
Higginson, well known literary figure, and William S. Scarborough, then president of Wilberforce College and a recognized Greek scholar and textbook writer. Scarborough and
Allen were Negroes.*

N. P. ROGERS [1]

The fugitive Douglass was up when we entered. This is an
extraordinary man. He was cut out for a hero. In a rising for Liberty, he would have been a Toussaint or a Hamilton. He has the
"heart to conceive, the head to contrive, and the hand to execute."

[1] From N. P. Rogers, "Herald of Freedom, Dec. 3, 1841," *Newspaper Writings*
(Concord, New Hampshire: John R. French, 1847), pp. 203–4.

A commanding person—over six feet, we should say, in height, and of most manly proportions. His head would strike a phrenologist amid a sea of them in Exeter Hall, and his voice would ring like a trumpet in the field. Let the South congratulate herself that he is a *fugitive*. It would not have been safe for her if he had remained about the plantations a year or two longer. Douglass is his *fugitive* name. He did not wear it in slavery. We don't know why he assumed it, or who bestowed it on him—but there seems *fitness* in it, to his commanding figure and heroic port. As a speaker he has few equals. It is not declamation—but oratory, power of debate. He watches the tide of discussion with the eye of the veteran, and dashes into it at once with all the tact of the forum or the bar. He has wit, argument, sarcasm, pathos—all that first-rate men show in their master efforts. His voice is highly melodious and rich, and his enunciation quite elegant, and yet he has been but two or three years out of the house of bondage. We noticed that he had strikingly improved, since we heard him at Dover in September. We say thus much of him, for he is esteemed by our multitude as of an inferior race. We should like to see him before any New England legislature or bar, and let him feel the freedom of the anti-slavery meeting, and see what would become of his inferiority. Yet he is a *thing*, in American estimate. He is the chattel of some pale-faced tyrant. How his owner would cower and shiver to hear him thunder in an anti-slavery hall! How he would shrink away, with his infernal whip, from his flaming eye when kindled with anti-slavery emotion! And the brotherhood of thieves, the *posse comitatus* of divines, we wish a hecatomb or two of the proudest and flintiest of them, were obliged to hear him thunder for human liberty, and lay the enslavement of his people at their doors. They would tremble like Belshazzar.

WILLIAM G. ALLEN [2]

In versatility of oratorical power, I know of no one who can begin to approach the celebrated Frederick Douglass. He, in very

[2] From " 'Orators and Orations,' an Address by William G. Allen before the Dialexian Society of New York Central College, June 22, 1852," *The Liberator* (Boston), October 29, 1852; also in *Frederick Douglass' Paper*, October 22, 1852.

deed, sways a magic wand. In the ability to imitate, he stands almost alone and unapproachable; and there is no actor living, whether he be tragedian or comedian, who would not give the world for such a face as his. His slaveholder's sermon is a masterpiece in its line. When he rises to speak, there is a slight hesitancy in his manner, which disappears as he warms up to his subject. He works with the power of a mighty intellect, and in the vast audiences which he never fails to assemble, touches chords in the inner chambers thereof which vibrate music now sweet, now sad, now lightsome, now solemn, now startling, now grand, now majestic, now sublime. He has a voice of terrific power, of great compass, and under most admirable control. Douglass is not only great in oratory, tongue-wise, but, considering his circumstances in early life, still more marvellous in composition, pen-wise. He has no fear of man; is no abstractionalist; he has a first-rate philosophy of reform; believes the boy would never have learned to swim if he had not gone near the water; and is consequently, particularly obnoxious to tavern keepers and steamboat captains, and those in general who mix up character and color, man and skin—and to all, in short, who have little hearts and muddy heads. He is the pride of the colored man and the terror of slaveholders and their abettors. Long may he live—an honor to his age, his race, his country and the world. . . .

THOMAS WENTWORTH HIGGINSON [3]

I spoke once before, but not so fully as I wished, of the man who on the anti-slavery platform, from his combination of the two races, was most interesting and most commanding for a time, though not always—for he differed from the others in detail and was more of a voting abolitionist than they were—Frederick Douglass.

In later years I walked once with Frederick Douglass through the streets of Worcester. It was the middle of winter and he wore a leopard-skin coat and cap. I well remember looking at him as he towered above my head and saying to myself:

[3] From Thomas Wentworth Higginson, *American Orators and Oratory* (Cleveland: Imperial Press, 1901), pp. 87–89.

"Make the most of this opportunity. You never before have walked the streets with so distinguished-looking a man, and you never will again." And I never have.

This man whom I had seen rise out of this clumsy lingering of the slavery manner, shot up into a superb man. This man, who learned originally to write from the placards in the Baltimore streets after he was eighteen, and by paying a little boy with an apple to tell him what certain letters were—this man gained such a command of speech and language that Mr. Yerrington, then the leading reporter of Boston, who always reported the anti-slavery meetings, told me that of all the speakers in those meetings, there were but two who could be reported without verbal alteration precisely as they spoke, and those two were Wendell Phillips and Frederick Douglass—the representative of the patrician training on the one side, and the representative of the Maryland slave on the other.

The tact of the man, the address of the man, and the humor of the man made him almost irresistible on the platform. He always had this proud bearing, and yet he was a perfect mimic. He could reproduce anything; he could meet any occasion. I remember him once at a convention in New York. The meeting had been overpowered by Captain Rynders, who was then the head of the swell mob in New York. He had taken possession of the meeting, had placed himself in the chair and graciously allowed the meeting to go on under his presidency. He had tried in vain to stop Douglass and check him, and had fallen back upon brutal interruptions, even saying, for instance, "Oh, you want to cut all our throats!"

"Oh, no," said the superb Douglass, bending down graciously over him and waving his hand a little over Rynders's tangled and soiled headdress, "Oh, no, we will not cut your throats; we will only cut your hair." And the supporters of Rynders felt the situation as much as anybody. I speak of Douglass the more because he has as yet left no rival of his type. Even Booker Washington, with all his remarkable qualities and undoubtedly an organizing power which Douglass had not, and perhaps destined in the end to be a more visibly useful man, has not that supreme power over an audience which Douglass had.

WILLIAM S. SCARBOROUGH [4]

Mr. Douglass's superior ability as an orator and as a writer was early recognized by the friends of the race, and from that day to this his services in behalf of his people have ever been in demand. On the other hand he has been ready to sacrifice his own best interests for his race, and he has not failed to make the sacrifice. He is a brilliant orator, a fluent talker, and an interesting conversationalist. He has an excellent memory, and can recall dates and facts of history with perfect ease. A day in his society is a rare treat, a privilege that might well be coveted by America's greatest citizens. The greatness of the man and the inspiration that comes from every word that he utters, make one wonder how it was possible for such a remarkable character to have ever been a slave, and, further, how even now it is possible for any discourtesies to be shown him because of his color. It is nevertheless true, however, that this distinguished American citizen must suffer with the rest of his fellows and share like indignities—and all because of his race. . . .

The cause of the oppressed could not have found a more eloquent defender than Mr. Douglass. Himself oppressed and denied the rights and privileges of a freeman, he felt what he said and said what he felt. The Negro's cause was his cause, and his cause was the Negro's cause. In defending his people he was defending himself. It was here that the brilliancy of his oratorical powers was most manifest. It was here that he was most profoundly eloquent. . . .

The scathing invectives and fiery eloquence of Mr. Douglass were the inevitable outcome of a soul longing for freedom in all that the term implies, not only for himself but for an oppressed race. His sole purpose was to stir the hearts of the American people against the system of slavery and color prejudice; to touch the philanthropic chord of the nation so as to induce it to recognize the brotherhood of man and the fatherhood of God. A tremendous task was his, but he never gave up the struggle. Day and night he pleaded for freedom, for citizenship, for equality of rights, for justice, for humanity. Could a higher sentiment of philanthropy and patriotism pervade a human soul than this?

[4] From William S. Scarborough, "Introduction," in James M. Gregory, *Frederick Douglass: The Orator* (Springfield, Mass.: Willey and Company, 1893), pp. 8–12.

13

Cayuga Chief: Champion of the African Race[1]

The role of spokesman for the Negro came to Douglass early in his public career, unsought but not unwelcome. In the spring of 1849, a reporter from an upstate New York newspaper took note of his abilities and of the Negro leadership role he had already come to assume in the eyes of white America.

Frederick Douglass addressed the people of this city last Thursday evening upon the subject of American Slavery. We listened to him for the first time and with a gratification seldom felt. From the reputation of the man as an able and eloquent champion of the African race, we were led to expect much; we were not disappointed. And while so many people are heaping opprobrium upon an injured people, we are glad to award the meed of praise to so gifted a representative.

The house is crowded. Cool and possessed, the black man eloquent sits. A pleasant air rests upon his countenance, tinged with the slightest possible shade of sarcasm. His eye, full, deep and restless, moves rapidly over the crowd, and glitters in the lamp lights like stars on the brow of night, while his head turns with the careless abandon of conscious strength.

His rise is unstudied, but not ungraceful. He rests his hands folded upon the pulpit cushion, and commences. His voice is low, but musical, hushing the still gathering crowd as the clearly enunciated sentences fall upon the ear. His manner is deliberate, and every

[1] From *Cayuga Chief* (Auburn, N. Y.), in *The Liberator* (Boston), April 20, 1849.

word is appropriate and fitly chosen, and the periods rounded with all the beauty and polish of a master.

As he proceeds, his voice gathers strength and volume. An intellect is there of no ordinary strength, although wrapped in a sable shroud. An engine is at work beneath that bushy crest, and the slow, measured strokes indicate that the fire is kindling rapidly. The rumble of thunder is heard, and the listener knows that storms are there. He warms as he moves on, and while watching the gathering blackness, it comes with a crash, alternately scathing and blighting and drenching obnoxious principles and obnoxious men. While the audience are watching the bold flight of the eagle in the cloud, they are startled at the roar of his swoop, and see his prey crushed and bleeding in his talons. His eyes flash, and the words fall warm and life-like from his lips. The same withering smile like the lightning glancing upon the ragged edges of the storm cloud, wreathes the face, save when his fierce invective, like a driving sleet, bursts indignantly from the heart. He handles his voice like a master. His under jaw protrudes when the heavier tones roll from the throat, as if crowded by them. His enunciation is perfectly distinct, and his language is classically chaste, not groaning under the flowery ornaments of school boy declamation, but terse yet eloquent, like a piece of finished sculpture beautiful in every outline of its symmetrical and unadorned simplicity.

We do not overrate the African. He is a swarthy Ajax, and with ponderous mace, he springs into the midst of his white oppressors and crushes them at every blow. With an air of scorn he hurls his bolts on every hand. He feels his wrongs, and his heart is in every blow.

Douglass is a master of every weapon. His powers of ridicule are great. Woe to the man or to the church whose hypocrisy passes in review.

His address was confined to the subject of prejudice against color. It was sometimes very severe, especially upon the churches which while proclaiming that of one flesh and blood God made all nations, and calling upon Ethiopia to partake free salvation of a God who is no respecter of persons, yet rear around the communion of a common Savior a black and a white table!

Many complain that he abuses churches and politicians. All deserved. They do not remember that Frederick Douglass is one of a proscribed and degraded people—that his heart burns under the wrongs heaped upon them by a Republic of Christians—that the whites brand them as inferior, ignorant and vicious—that they have no voice in a government that demands its pound of flesh of them —that they are outlawed, while aliens of European Despotisms are flooded upon our shores, and transformed into American citizens— that they toil in slavery to enrich a Nation that grinds them into dust—that they are barricaded from the schools of our land and of every chance of moral and intellectual improvement.

We wonder not that Frederick Douglass is severe. We applaud him for his boldness. We like to see a man stand erect and plead for himself and his race and for truth, although blood may drip from his blade. Our own shoulders may bleed, but we do admire a fearless arm.

Douglass is logical. His review of Clay's letter upon Emancipation was close, severe, and annihilating. Not one who heard it could say otherwise.

Douglass is a strong man.

14

William Lloyd Garrison:
A Volley from a Former Friend[1]

In matters of strategy and tactics the anti-slavery reformers frequently held sharply differing viewpoints, and on occasion their quarrels were characterized by a great bitterness of spirit. Such was the case of the irreparable breach that developed between Douglass and William Lloyd Garrison. In the early 1840's the two reformers had been very close associates, touring together the anti-slavery circuit at home and abroad. But when Douglass started to publish a newspaper of his own, ignoring Garrison's advice, the latter grew cool toward his former protegé. Garrison's hostility mounted in 1851, when Douglass announced himself a voting abolitionist, a stance which ran counter to Garrison's contention that participation in political party activity was unsound in theory and doubtful in morality. The breach between the former friends was widened by the factor of race. No man in ante-bellum America was more beloved by Negroes than Garrison, and he in turn showed great regard for them. But, however liberal his racial outlook, Garrison was not wholly immune from the spirit of condescension toward colored people so pervasive in his day. Hence for a Negro, and a former slave at that, to quit his ranks and then proceed to criticize him in sharp tones was too much even for a Garrison. In a lead editorial in the December 16, 1853, issue of The Liberator, *Garrison let fly at Douglass, winding up with a reference to Julia Griffiths, an Englishwoman who had come to America expressly to assist Douglass in his anti-slavery activities.*

[1] *The Liberator* (Boston), December 16, 1853.

THE MASK ENTIRELY REMOVED

> "Either he must
> Confess himself wondrous malicious,
> Or be accused of folly."—CORIOLANUS.

In his paper of the 9th instant, Frederick Douglass occupies twelve columns in reply to sundry brief articles in the *Pennsylvania Freeman, Anti-Slavery Standard; Bugle,* and *Liberator,* respecting his feelings and attitude towards his old friends and associates in the cause of emancipation. Such portions of it as relate to the other journals referred to, we leave them to dispose of as they may think proper. We quote all that is personal to us, in addition to a considerable portion of Mr. D.'s exordium; and from this sample, our readers can easily infer what the remainder must be.

The history of the Anti-Slavery struggle has been marked by instances of defection, alienation, apostacy, on the part of some of its most efficient supporters for a given time; but by none more signal, venomous, or extraordinary, than the present. Mr. Douglass now stands self-unmasked, his features flushed with passion, his air scornful and defiant, his language bitter as wormwood, his pen dipped in poison; as thoroughly changed in his spirit as was ever "arch-angel ruined," and as artful and unscrupulous a schismatic as has yet appeared in the abolition ranks.

Having long endeavored, by extreme forbearance, to avoid any collision with him; having omitted in many cases to make even a passing reference to what we deemed unworthy of his position; having criticised, with brevity and moderation, some very objectionable articles from his pen, only because we could not be true to our convictions of duty, if we suppressed the expression of our surprise and sorrow; and having no feelings of personal animosity to gratify; we have no intention to make a protracted rejoinder in the present case, but shall submit the whole matter, in a very few words, to the impartial judgment of all who take any interest in the controversy.

It is difficult to believe that the author of the article of "enormous" length and character, now under consideration, is the Frederick Douglass once so manly, generous, and faithful. The transformation

—or, rather, the revelation—is the most astounding and severely painful event in our experience; and "the end is not yet." He now assumes an attitude which is eliciting the warmest encomiums from the most malignant enemies of the Anti-Slavery movement, and which is undisguisedly hostile to his old companion in arms. No marvel, therefore, that he can speak of the "Garrisonians" with as much flippancy as any of our pro-slavery contemners; or that he can aver, "*Word*-wise, these Garrisonians are my best friends—*deed*-wise, I have no more vigilant enemies"; or that he is able to say of the "REFUGE OF OPPRESSION," that, "of late, it has become about the best part of Mr. Garrison's paper, and about which nobody cares a single straw"; or that he can utter the monstrous untruth, that "a fierce and bitter warfare" is waged against him, "under the general-ship of William Lloyd Garrison," with a view to destroy *his anti-slavery usefulness!!*

The untruthfulness of Mr. D. is matched only by his adroitness in striving to excite popular sympathy, as though he were a poor inno-cent lamb, about to be torn in pieces by a pack of famished wolves! Though he is the aggressor, he affects to have made no effort even in self-defence, and whiningly says—"I shall be silent no longer(!) The impunity allowed to my adversaries, by my silence, like all other submission to wrong, has failed to soften the heart of the wrong-doers(!) They have waxed more arrogant as I have waxed humble"(!) "Gerrit Smith is an independent nation. Alas! I am but a rebel. While those against whom I have rebelled would treat with Mr. Smith, they would hang me." Again—"I had reason to know that prejudice against color—yes, prejudice against my race, would be invoked, as it has been invoked, on the side of my adver-saries(!)—and in all the likelihoods of the case, the question be-tween me and my old friends would be decided in this case as between white and black—in favor of the former, and against the latter—the white man to rise, as an injured benefactor, and the black man to fall, as a miserable ingrate"(!) Again—"The specta-cle of a rich(!) and powerful(!) organization, largely provided with the appliances of moral warfare, is now seen marshalling its forces, its presses, and its speakers, for the moral extermination of one hum-ble, solitary individual(!!!)—for the purpose of silencing, and put-ting to open shame, *a fugitive slave,*(!) simply because that fugitive

slave has dared to differ from that Society, or from the leading individuals in it, as to the manner in which he shall exercise his powers
for the promotion of the anti-slavery cause, and the elevation of
the free people of color in the United States"(!!) Again—"The
hatchet of fratricidal war is uplifted; nay, it is now flung at the head
of its appointed victim, with the combined force of three strong
arms, and with the deadly aim of three good marksmen"(!!!) And
this is his estimate of the American Anti-Slavery Society, its presses,
and its speakers! Now, as a specimen of low cunning and malignant
defamation, we have never seen this surpassed. It is too palpable to
need a single word in reply, and we should be lost to all self-respect
to treat it as worthy of serious consideration.

Mr. Douglass sneers at the regret expressed by us, and others, at
the necessity of noticing his hostile assaults, and scoffingly says—
"They have had to overcome mountains of reluctance in getting at
me; and it is amazing, considering the ruggedness of these mountains, that they ever succeeded in crossing their Alpine heights!"
If this does not indicate either that we have never, in his opinion,
been his true friends, or that, ever selfish and untrue himself, he is
incapable of experiencing the pang of misplaced confidence and
disappointed friendship, we know not how to interpret language.
In either case, it places him in a most unenviable position.

Jaundiced in vision, and inflamed with passion, he affects to
regard us as the "disparager"(!) of the colored race, and artfully
endeavors to excite their jealousy and opposition by utterly perverting the meaning of our language. We said, that "the Anti-Slavery
cause, both religiously and politically, has transcended the ability
of the sufferers from American slavery and prejudice, *as a class,* to
keep pace with it, or to perceive what are its demands, or to understand the philosophy of its operations"—meaning by this, that the
cause requires religious and political sacrifices, which, "as a class,"
they do not yet see, or, seeing, are not yet prepared to make, even
though they are the victims to be delivered—and also meaning that
what was at first supposed to be local, is now seen to have a world-
wide bearing, and must be advocated upon world-wide principles,
irrespective of complexional differences. There is nothing really or
intentionally invidious in a statement like this: and yet, how does

Mr. Douglass treat it? "The colored man," he says, "ought to feel profoundly grateful for this magnificent compliment to their high moral worth and breadth of comprehension, so generously bestowed by William Lloyd Garrison! Who will doubt, hereafter, the *natural* inferiority of the Negro, when the great champion of the Negroes' rights *thus broadly concedes all that is claimed respecting the Negro's inferiority by the bitterest despisers of the Negro race" !!!* Now, if this were blundering stupidity, it might readily be pardoned; but it is unmitigated baseness, and therefore inexcusable.

Again we said—"It does not follow, that, because a man is or has been a slave, or because he is identified with a class meted out and trodden under foot, therefore he will be the truest to the cause of human freedom"—a truism which nothing can make plainer. Yet Mr. Douglass presumes upon the color of his skin to vindicate his superior fidelity to that cause, and to screen himself from criticism and rebuke! This trick cannot succeed. Of the colored people he says—"What is theory to others, is practice to them. Every day and hour is crowded with lessons to them on the subject, to which the whites, as a class, are strangers." Very true—but what then? Does it indicate the same regard for universal justice, for those who are oppressed to desire to gain their freedom, as it does for others, not of their complexion, and not involved in their suffering, to encounter deadly perils and make liberal sacrifices in seeking their liberation? The former may be animated by motives limited to a narrow selfishness; the latter must be actuated by feelings of disinterested benevolence and world-wide philanthropy. Once, Mr. Douglass would have promptly recognized this distinction; now, beneath the blackness of his skin he is attempting to hide the blackness of his treachery.

How low he has fallen is further indicated by his despicable insinuation—"Even Charles L. Remond, who was scarcely recognized as one of the 'tried' and 'true,' *when poor,* has, *since making himself well off by marriage,* rapidly risen in Boston favor"! Is not this at once the acme of absurdity, the extreme of falsehood, and the lowest depth of moral debasement? When Frederick Douglass was "poor," and in utter obscurity, and not as now every where visible, was *he* a stranger to "Boston favor," and was nothing done to raise him up to respectability and influence? But this is to hint that he is destitute of grateful emotions—and gratitude is something about which he does not like to be reminded.

A word in regard to our allusion to a bad adviser in Mr. D.'s printing-office, whom we accused of exerting a pernicious influence upon his mind and judgment, and "causing much unhappiness in his own household." That last allusion was not meant unkindly, nor intended to imply any thing immoral; but, though it is strictly true, and we could bring a score of unimpeachable witnesses in Rochester to prove it, we regret it was made, as it had no relevancy. Our only object in referring to that nameless "adviser" was, to indicate to such inquirers as our Chicago correspondent, that there had been secret causes at work to alienate Mr. Douglass from his old associates, and we felt bound to throw out the intimation as a clue to much that would be otherwise inexplicable to those not familiar with the facts in the case. Mr. D. says—"I am profoundly grateful for the eminent services of that 'adviser,' in *opening my eyes*(!) to many things connected with my anti-slavery relations, to which I had before been partially blind." That tells the whole story, and is all we care to extort. In what condition his vision now is —and whether in slumbering in the lap of a prejudiced, sectarian Delilah, he has not at last enabled the pro-slavery Philistines to ascertain the secret of his strength, cut off his locks, and rejoice over his downfall—we leave our readers and the uncompromising friends of the Anti-Slavery cause to judge.

15

J. McCune Smith:
A Representative American[1]

The second autobiography of Douglass, My Bondage and My Freedom, *published in 1855, carried an "Introduction" by J. McCune Smith, holder of three degrees from the
University of Glasgow. Despite a large medical practice in
New York, Smith had become the city's leading Negro in reformist movements and civic affairs. In his introduction to
the book, Smith attributed the importance of Douglass to his
Americanism—to his being "a type of his countrymen." Smith
was a persuasive writer, in style and in substance.*

The life of Frederick Douglass, recorded in the pages which
follow, is not merely an example of self-elevation under the most
adverse circumstances; it is, moreover, a noble vindication of the
highest aims of the American anti-slavery movement. The real
object of that movement is not only to disenthrall, it is, also, to
bestow upon the Negro the exercise of all those rights, from the
possession of which he has been so long debarred.

But this full recognition of the colored man to the right, and
the entire admission of the same to the full privileges, political,
religious and social, of manhood, requires powerful effort on the
part of the enthralled, as well as on the part of those who would
disenthrall them. The people at large must feel the conviction,
as well as admit the abstract logic, of human equality; the Negro,
for the first time in the world's history, brought in full contact with
high civilization, must prove his title to all that is demanded for

[1] From J. McCune Smith, "Introduction," in Frederick Douglass, *My Bondage
and My Freedom* (New York: Miller, Orton and Mulligan, 1855), pp. xvii-xviii,
xxv-xxvi, xxvii-xxix, xxxi.

him; in the teeth of unequal chances, he must prove himself equal to the mass of those who oppress him—therefore, absolutely superior to his apparent fate, and to their relative ability. And it is most cheering to the friends of freedom, today, that evidence of this equality is rapidly accumulating, not from the ranks of the half-freed colored people of the free states, but from the very depths of slavery itself; the indestructible equality of man to man is demonstrated by the ease with which black men, scarce one remove from barbarism—if slavery can be honored with such a distinction—vault into the high places of the most advanced and painfully acquired civilization. . . .

It has been said in this Introduction, that Mr. Douglass had raised himself by his own efforts to the highest position in society. As a successful editor, in our land, he occupies this position. Our editors rule the land, and he is one of them. As an orator and thinker, his position is equally high, in the opinion of his countrymen. If a stranger in the United States would seek its most distinguished men—the movers of public opinion—he will find their names mentioned, and their movements chronicled, under the head of "BY MAGNETIC TELEGRAPH," in the daily papers. The keen caterers for the public attention, set down, in this column, such men only as have won high mark in the public esteem. During the past winter—1854–5—very frequent mention of Frederick Douglass was made under this head in the daily papers; his name glided as often—this week from Chicago, next week from Boston—over the lightning wires, as the name of any other man, of whatever note. To no man did the people more widely nor more earnestly say, *"Tell me thy thought!"* And, somehow or other, revolution seemed to follow in his wake. His were not the mere words of eloquence which Kossuth speaks of, that delight the ear and then pass away. No! They were *work*-able, *do*-able words, that brought forth fruits in the revolution in Illinois, and in the passage of the franchise resolutions by the Assembly of New York.

And the secret of his power, what is it? He is a Representative American man—a type of his countrymen. Naturalists tell us that a full grown man is a resultant or representative of all animated nature on this globe; beginning with the early embryo state, then representing the lowest forms of organic life, and passing through every subordinate grade or type, until he reaches the last and highest—manhood. In like manner, and to the fullest extent, has Frederick Douglass passed through every gradation of rank comprised in our national make-up, and bears upon his person and upon his soul every thing that is American. And he has not only full sympathy with every thing American; his proclivity or bent, to active toil and visible progress, are in the strictly national direction, delighting to outstrip "all creation."

Nor have the natural gifts, already named as his, lost anything by his severe training. When unexcited, his mental processes are probably slow, but singularly clear in perception, and wide in vision, the unfailing memory bringing up all the facts in their every aspect; incongruities he lays hold of incontinently, and holds up on the edge of his keen and telling wit. But this wit never descends to frivolity; it is rigidly in the keeping of his truthful common sense, and always used in illustration or proof of some point which could not so readily be reached any other way. "Beware of a Yankee when he is feeding," is a shaft that strikes home in a matter never so laid bare by satire before. . . .

"The man who is right is a majority," is an aphorism struck out by Mr. Douglass in that great gathering of the friends of freedom, at Pittsburgh, in 1852, where he towered among the highest, because, with abilities inferior to none, and moved more deeply than any, there was neither policy nor party to trammel the outpourings of his soul. Thus we find, opposed to all the disadvantages which a black man in the United States labors and struggles under, is this one vantage ground—when the chance comes, and the audience where he may have a say, he stands forth the freest, most deeply moved and most earnest of all men.

It has been said of Mr. Douglass, that his descriptive and declamatory powers, admitted to be of the very highest order, take precedence of his logical force. Whilst the schools might have trained him to the exhibition of the formulas of deductive logic, nature and circumstances forced him into the exercise of the higher faculties required by induction. The first ninety pages of this *Life in Bondage,* afford specimens of observing, comparing, and careful classifying, of such superior character, that it is difficult to believe them the results of a child's thinking; he questions the earth, and the children and the slaves around him again and again, and finally looks to *"God in the sky"* for the why and the wherefore of the unnatural thing, slavery. *"Yere, if indeed thou art, wherefore dost thou suffer us to be slain?"* is the only prayer and worship of the God-forsaken Dodos in the heart of Africa. Almost the same was his prayer. One of his earliest observations was that white children should know their ages, while the colored children were ignorant of theirs; and the songs of the slaves grated on his inmost soul, because a something told him that harmony in sound, and music of the spirit, could not consociate with miserable degradation.

To such a mind, the ordinary processes of logical deduction are like proving that two and two make four. Mastering the intermediate steps by an intuitive glance, or recurring to them as Ferguson resorted to geometry, it goes down to the deeper relation of things, and brings out what may seem, to some, mere statements, but which are new and brilliant generalizations, each resting on a broad and stable basis. Thus, Chief Justice Marshall gave his decisions, and then told Brother Story to look up the authorities— and they never differed from him. Thus, also, in his "Lecture on the Anti-Slavery Movement," delivered before the Rochester Ladies' Anti-Slavery Society, Mr. Douglass presents a mass of thought, which, without any showy display of logic on his part, requires an exercise of the reasoning faculties of the reader to keep pace with him. And his "Claims of the Negro Ethnologically Considered," is full of new and fresh thoughts on the dawning science of race-history. . . .

The most remarkable mental phenomenon in Mr. Douglass, is his style in writing and speaking. In March, 1855, he delivered an address in the assembly chamber before the members of the legislature of the state of New York. An eye witness [William H. Topp, of Albany] describes the crowded and most intelligent audience, and their rapt attention to the speaker, as the grandest scene he ever witnessed in the capitol. Among those whose eyes were riveted on the speaker full two hours and a half, were Thurlow Weed and Lieutenant Governor Raymond; the latter, at the conclusion of the address, exclaimed to a friend, "I would give twenty thousand dollars, if I could deliver that address in that manner." Mr. Raymond is a first class graduate of Dartmouth, a rising politician, ranking foremost in the legislature; of course, his ideal of oratory must be of the most polished and finished description. . . .

It is not without a feeling of pride, dear reader, that I present you with this book. The son of a self-emancipated bond-woman, I feel joy in introducing to you my brother, who has rent his own bonds, and who, in his every relation—as a public man, as a husband and as a father—is such as does honor to the land which gave him birth. I shall place this book in the hands of the only child spared me, bidding him to strive and emulate its noble example. You may do likewise. It is an American book, for Americans, in the fullest sense of the idea. It shows that the worst of our institutions, in its worst aspect, cannot keep down energy, truthfulness, and earnest struggle for the right. It proves the justice and practicability of Immediate Emancipation. It shows that any man in our land, "no matter in what battle his liberty may have been cloven down, . . . no matter what complexion an Indian or an African sun may have burned upon him," not only may "stand forth redeemed and disenthralled," but may also stand up a candidate for the highest suffrage of a great people—the tribute of their honest, hearty admiration.   Reader, *Vale!*

New York, May 23, 1855.   JAMES M'CUNE SMITH.

16

John Edward Bruce:
Somewhat Less than a God

An outspoken critic himself, Douglass could not hope to enjoy immunity from dispraise. Inasmuch as Negroes were sometimes the object of his upbraiding, so were they to be numbered among his critics. Chief of these, in the 1880's, was John Edward Bruce, a newspaper editor and free-lance journalist who often wrote under the name of "Bruce Grit," and who, like Douglass, did not mince words. In the spring of 1889, Bruce criticized Douglass for remarks made in a speech celebrating the twenty-seventh anniversary of the abolition of slavery in the District of Columbia.

Mr. Frederick Douglass, in a speech delivered here [Washington, D. C.] on the 16th of April last, took occasion to advise the colored people of the United States against encouraging race pride, arguing that a solid black minority would tend to array the white people against us—intimating that we would come nearer to the solution of the problem by assimilating with the whites, etc., etc. This is Mr. Douglass' advice to the Negro. It is bad advice; it is one of Mr. Douglass' dreams, which he nor his posterity will hardly live to see realized. Mr. Douglass evidently wants to get away from the Negro race, and from the criticism I have heard quite recently of him, he will not meet with any armed resistance in his flight.

I also take exception to Mr. Douglass' animadversions upon certain colored journals, which he does not seem to have the courage to name. His attempts to belittle the colored press were worthy of a better cause. He owes much of his popularity to the colored fool

[1] From John Edward Bruce to the editor of the *Cleveland Gazette,* in *Cleveland Gazette,* May 11, 1889 and June 8, 1889.

editors around the country whose little patent inside and outside sheets have made him something less than a god, by keeping his name continually in their columns, and in endeavoring to convince ordinary mortals that when God created Frederick Douglass, He finished His work with the exception of the sun, moon and stars to reflect their rays upon him as he walked up and down the land. Mr. Douglass has courted their attention; he has coquetted with their editors, correspondents and reporters; he has used them to the extent of his ability; he has commended them as indispensable auxiliaries in the work of lifting the race to a higher plane in the social and intellectual world. And now that he sees or imagines that they can no longer be used, the question of their utility as helps in the solution of the Negro problem is disposed of by him with a slur and a contemptuous fling at their "youthful imperfections." Demosthenes said, "It becometh him who receiveth a benefit from another man, forever to be sensible to it," and Socrates said, "He is unjust who does not return deserved thanks for any benefit, whether the giver be friend or foe." Noble words, these, and fitly spoken. Mr. Douglass may not be able to discover at this time any thing in colored journalism worthy of his support and encouragement. His own failures as a journalist and publisher may have doubtless embittered him somewhat, but all colored journals are not failures. Many of them manage to exist without the yearly subscription of Frederick Douglass some way or another.

> "Ungenerous man, and hard of heart,
> Who takes the kind, and plays the ungrateful part."

Mr. Douglass comes back at my criticism of his desperately diplomatic bid for office,[2] to say that he freely grants me the mercy of his silence, at the same time intimating that he may not always grant me this gracious indulgence. This, in my judgment, is no answer to any thing I have said about his speech. I frankly confess that I fail to see the point he makes, unless it be that he wishes me to understand that if I shall have the hardihood to refer to him

[2] At the time Douglass was being considered for a diplomatic post. On July 1, 1889, shortly after Bruce's letters, Douglass's appointment as Minister-Resident and Consul-General to the Republic of Haiti was announced by President Harrison.

again he will attack me personally; and yet I cannot make myself believe that a man of Mr. Douglass' standing, whose immediate connections have not established the best reputation for veracity, and whose credibility as witnesses must of necessity be questioned, can afford to sneeringly allude to or threaten into silence, as he thinks, the voice of any man who differs from him on public questions. If this is Mr. Douglass' point he is welcome to all the consolation he can extract from a personal attack upon me. I do not fear his eloquence or his money, and I will defend myself vigorously and aggressively. Infallibility and personal holiness are as great strangers in the Douglass household as they are in those of ordinary mortals.

17

James D. Corrothers: Douglass in Sportive Mood[1]

Although one practically never sees a picture of Douglass smiling, he had a lively sense of humor that goes with not taking oneself too seriously. A young poet-author, James D. Corrothers, relates an incident in Chicago in 1893, which shows Douglass in a light mood. Douglass was winding up a seven-month-long appointment as Commissioner from Haiti to the Chicago World's Fair, and Corrothers wished to give him due recognition.

I conceived the idea of giving Mr. Douglass a great Farewell Public Reception which would give all classes of my race an opportunity to show that they honoured him as truly as did the whites; and to pour out their gratitude to him for all he had accomplished in their behalf. I wondered, when I came to think it over, why such a thing as a public testimonial of gratitude had never been given to him by his race in all his life. I talked the matter over with Mr. Douglass, and obtained his consent to my plan. "We young people in Chicago are going to honour you," I told him, "as you never were honoured before."

"O Corrothers," he replied laughingly, in that lion-like voice of his, "you don't know how much of that I can stand!"

[1] From James D. Corrothers, *In Spite of the Handicap* (New York: George H. Noran Company, 1916), p. 127. For an account of the reception see *ibid.*, pp. 127–33.

18
His Shining Example

The passing of Douglass in February, 1895, brought forth a deluge of eulogies which, characteristically, spoke only good of the dead. But some of them, despite the accents of praise, sought to evaluate the man and his significance. Of the following three selections the two in prose are by Francis J. Grimké, who had officiated at Douglass's second marriage in 1884, and Albion W. Tougée, former North Carolina Reconstruction judge and author of the best-selling novel, A Fool's Errand. The poetical selection is by the gifted Paul Laurence Dunbar, whom Douglass had befriended. Dunbar and Grimké were Negroes. In a lengthy book (In Memoriam: Frederick Douglass, Philadelphia, 1897), Douglass's widow brought together the most important of these eulogies, plus letters of condolence from prominent persons.

FRANCIS J. GRIMKÉ [1]

By nature he was cast in a great mould, physically, intellectually, morally.

Physically, what a splendid specimen of a man he was: tall, erect, massive, and yet moving with the grace and agility of an Apollo. How Phidias or Michelangelo would have delighted to chisel in marble, or cast in bronze that noble form and figure! It was always a pleasure to me just to look at him. His presence affected me like some of the passages of rugged grandeur in Milton, or as the sight of Mt. Blanc, rising from the vale of Chamouni, affected Coleridge, when for the first time he looked out upon that magnificent scene.

[1] From Francis J. Grimké, "Obituary Sermon, Fifteenth Street Presbyterian Church, Washington, D. C., March 10, 1895," in James M. Gregory, *Frederick Douglass: The Orator,* 2nd ed. (Springfield, Mass.: Willey and Company, 1895?), pp. 273–76, 292–96, 301–6, 309.

I think all who came in contact with him felt the spell of his splendid presence. The older he grew, the whiter his locks became, the more striking was his appearance, and the more did he attract attention wherever he appeared, whether on the street or in public gatherings. I was never more impressed with this fact than at the great Columbian Exposition in Chicago. One morning I had the pleasure of going with him to the Art Gallery. There were several things that he wanted to show me, he said. The first thing that we stopped before was a piece of statuary, "Lincoln Dying." We had been standing there but a short time before a crowd gathered about us. I was absorbed in what he was saying, and did not at first notice it, but he took in the situation at once, it was an old story to him, and said, "Well, they have come; let us pass on." And wherever we went in the building the same thing was repeated. It seemed as if nearly everybody knew him, but even those who did not know him were attracted by his remarkable appearance.

Intellectually, what a splendid specimen of a man he was! His intellect was of a very high order. He possessed a mind of remarkable acuteness and penetration, and of great philosophic grasp. It was wonderful how readily he resolved effects into their causes, and with what ease he got down to the underlying facts and principles of whatever subject he attempted to treat. Hence he was always a formidable antagonist to encounter. No man ever crossed swords with him who was not forced to acknowledge, even when he did not agree with him, his transcendent ability. He had the faculty of seeing at a glance the weak points in an opponent's position, and, with the skill of a trained dialectician, knew how to marshal all the arguments at his command, in the form of facts and principles, in refutation of the same. It was to me a constant delight to witness the play of his remarkable powers of mind as they came out in his great speeches and published articles. He had a strong, mighty intellect. They called him the Sage of Anacostia; and so he was—all that that term implies—wise, thoughtful, sound of judgment, discriminating, far-seeing.

Morally, what a splended specimen of a man he was—lofty in sentiment, pure in thought, exalted in character. Upon the loftiest plane of a pure and noble manhood he lived and moved. No one need ever be ashamed to call his name. There he stands, in the serene, beautiful white light of a virtuous manhood! For more than fifty years he was before the public eye: not infrequently during that time he was the object of the bitterest hatred, and yet during all those years, in the face of the strongest opposition, with the worst passions arrayed against him, no one dared even to whisper anything derogatory of him, or in any way reflecting upon the purity of his life, or upon the honesty and integrity of his character. There have been among us, in the past history of our race, men who were richly endowed intellectually, and who, like him, possessed also that rarest of gifts, the mighty gift of eloquence—men who could hold entranced great audiences by the hour, the fame of whose eloquence has come down to us; but when you have said that of them, you have said all. Beyond that, you dare not go. When it comes to character, which infinitely transcends in point of value all mere intellectual endowments, or even the gift of eloquence, we are obliged to hang our heads, and remain silent, or go backward and cover their shame. But not so here. No one need ever hang his head when the name of Frederick Douglass is mentioned, or feel the necessity of silence. . . .

He consecrated to the service of his race, his time and all the powers of his body and mind. He labored incessantly; he was instant in season and out of season; he worked by day and by night; he was at it, and always at it. The wonder is that even his iron constitution did not break down under the strain. He himself tells us that he used to write all day, and then take the train and go off at night and speak, returning the same evening or early the next morning, only to resume his work at his desk. . . .

Some men have said: "Douglass was selfish; he always had an eye to his own interest," implying that it was not the race that he was thinking about so much as of himself. For this base insinuation, for that is the only term which properly characterizes it, I have the utmost contempt. When I think of how richly this man was endowed; of the great services which he rendered to freedom, and remember that his salary was only four hundred and fifty dollars a year; when I think of his self-sacrificing efforts to carry on his paper, *The North Star*, putting every cent he could into it, even mortgaging the house over his head, I say I do not believe it. I have

read his life carefully; and I had the honor of knowing him in-
timately for a number of years; and as I look back over those
years, I can recall nothing that would in any way justify such an
accusation. . . .

There are many other things that might be mentioned under
the general head which we are considering, but time will not
permit. Suffice it to say that during the last fifty years of his life
there was no measure looking to the betterment of our condition,
as a people in this country, in which he was not a leading actor.
For fifty years he allowed no opportunity to pass unimproved in
which, either by his voice or pen, he could make the way easier
and the future brighter for this race. Whenever we needed a defender, he was always on hand. Whenever there were rights to be
asserted, he always stood ready to make the demand: never lagging
behind, always at the front. For over fifty years he stood as the
sentinel on the watch-tower, guarding with the most jealous care
the interest of this race. I remember how I felt when he was
appointed Minister to Haiti. I did not want him to go, and I wrote
and told him so, and told him why. It was because I felt that we
could not spare him out of the country. It seemed to me our
interests would not be quite so safe if he were away. The very fact
that he was here filled me with the assurance that all would be well.
And that is the way I think we all felt—a sense of security in the
consciousness of the fact that Great Douglass was in our midst. . . .

I would like to speak of some of his personal traits and characteristics—of his gentleness, his sympathetic nature, his tenderness,
his generosity, his great-heartedness. There was nothing mean or
close-fisted or penurious about him. God blessed him with means,
and he used it for the glory of his Maker and the good of his
fellow men. He was all the time giving to some good cause or
reaching out the helping hand to the needy. Years ago, when there
was a movement to purchase a building for the use of the Colored
Young Men's Christian Association in the city of Washington, made
necessary because they were shut out of the white association, in
company with the International Secretary, Mr. Hunton, we called
upon him and laid the matter before him. He listened to us, and
when we were through said: "Gentlemen, I am not a rich man;

I can't give you as large a subscription as I would like to, but I will do something. Put me down for two hundred dollars." And that is but a sample of what he was constantly doing.

In the city of Baltimore, some years before he made his escape from slavery, while he was working in one of the shipyards, he was set upon by some white laborers, was mobbed, dreadfully beaten, and came very near losing his life. The cry was, "Kill the nigger!" Among those who responded to that cry and who tried hard to kill him was a man who, up to a short time before Mr. Douglass' death, was still alive and living in Baltimore. He was then old, sick, decrepit and in great destitution. Mr. Douglass heard of it while in Baltimore, called upon him, spoke kindly to him and, in parting, left a ten-dollar note in his hand. It was a beautiful, a gracious thing for him to do, but it was just like him. He was all the time doing noble things. God bless his memory and give us more men like him.

I might also speak of his love of the beautiful in art and in nature. At the great Columbian Exposition the Art Gallery was a constant delight to him. He reveled in its treasures. He loved also all nature —the flowers, and the grass, and the trees, and the birds, and the drifting clouds, and the blue sky, and the stars. He had a poet's love of nature. With Wordsworth he could say:

> "To me the meanest flower that blows can give
> Thoughts that do often lie too deep for tears."

How often have I heard him speak, as I have sat with him on the front porch of his beautiful home in Anacostia, or under the trees on the hillside, with the lovely landscape stretching out on all sides around us, of the pleasure which it gave him, the satisfaction, of how it rested him to commune with nature. . . .

To those of us who are members of the race with which he was identified, I would say: "Let us keep his shining example ever before us. Let each one of us endeavor to catch his noble spirit; to walk upon the same lofty plain of a pure and exalted manhood upon which he moved: and together, in the consciousness of the fact that he is no longer with us, let us consecrate ourselves anew with what powers we may possess to the furtherance of the great cause to which he gave his life."

And may I not also, in his name, appeal to the members of the dominant race, especially to those who revere his memory, to join with us in continuing to fight for the great principles for which he contended until in all sections of this fair land there shall be equal opportunities for all, irrespective of race, color or previous condition of servitude until, to borrow the language of another, "Character, not color, shall stamp the man and woman." And when black and white shall clasp friendly hands, in the consciousness of the fact that we are all brothers, and that God is the Father of us all.

ALBION W. TOURGÉE [2]

The life we commemorate to-night was, in some respects, among the most remarkable the world has ever known. In sharp and swift recurring contrasts it has never been excelled. In the distance from its beginning to its ending it has rarely been equalled. If a man's capacity be measured by what he achieved, Frederick Douglass must be ranked among the great men of a great day; if by the obstacles overcome, he must be accounted among the greatest of any time.

Historical Parallel

In all history there is but one parallel of his career, and that one lacks the most important element. Twenty-five hundred years ago a slave so won upon his master's love and pride that he was set free. The most cultivated people in ancient history hung upon his words in admiration. Their philosophers imitated his methods; their poets parodied his fables. He became the friend, counsellor, and ambassador of the greatest king of his time. When he died Athens voted him a statue, and four cities claimed the honor of

[2] From Albion W. Tourgée, "The Eulogy," delivered in Faneuil Hall, Boston, December 20, 1895, in *A Memorial of Frederick Douglass from the City of Boston* (Boston: Printed by order of the City Council, 1896), pp. 27–30, 65–67.

being accounted his birthplace. He is said to have been a hunch-
back, and this fact is always cited as evidence of his transcendent
genius because of the added burden it imposed. He had not only
to overcome the prejudice attaching to his station, but also the
aversion inspired by his uncouthness. The schoolboy of to-day, as
he cons this story, wonders how he could rise to such heights in
the face of such obstacles, especially among a beauty-loving people
like the Athenians.

Yet, what were the difficulties in the way of Æsop compared
with those which Douglass overcame? What was Grecian bondage
in comparison with American slavery? What was Æsop's hump
when compared with Douglass' color, considered as an obstacle to
personal success? What was the patronage of Crœsus to the friendship of Lincoln and Grant, Sumner and Garrison, Whittier and
Phillips—and all the unnumbered host of good men and women
to whom Douglass' name became a household word and in whose
homes he was a welcome guest? No slave was ever before so potent
in the counsels of freemen. No Negro ever before became so widely
and favorably known among an Anglo-Saxon people. . . .

Three classes of the American people are under special obligations
to him: the colored bondman whom he helped to free from the
chains which he himself had worn; the free persons of color whom
he helped to make citizens; the white people of the United States
whom he sought to free from the bondage of caste and relieve from
the odium of slavery. . . .

The Lesson of His Life

His memory should be an inspiration to every colored man and a
warning to every white American that caste discrimination, whether
it be the prop of slavery or other wrong, cannot long be justified by
its results. While it may be many years or even generations before
another colored man will attain the same distinctive prominence in
the whole country, Mr. Douglass was not only the exponent of new
conditions but the exception that proves the rule in regard to old
ones. A people that can produce a Douglass under the conditions
that beset his life, will unquestionably produce many who shall be
his superiors in attainment and power under an improved environ-

ment. The law of the evolution of types in humanity is just as inflexible as in the lower orders of life. One Douglass born out of slavery is the forerunner of many to be born out of the semi-freedom which is all that Caste permits his race yet to enjoy.

The difficulties that beset his life can never be duplicated in all the world's life which is to be. One of the twin dragons of oppression has at least been slain. Slavery is no more. From the rising to the setting of the sun there is no place in any civilized land where oppression dare wear that name. The slave-ship, the slave-mart, the auction-block, the life which was in all things subject to another's will, the political condition which denied marriage and family, and legal offspring, which by law refused the rights of self-defence, forbade the race to possess or to inherit; to receive, to give or take; to sue or be sued; which denied the sacred rite of marriage, and in the name of Christ forced millions to an adulterous estate to gratify Christian lust and greed—this monster, which not only had survived the Dark Ages but grew daily more horrible in character and aspect with the advance of civilization, is at least no more! Not only in our land but in all the earth slavery is dead! Only the evil stench of its decay remains to offend the moral sense of man!

Caste, the twin demon, is yet to be destroyed. Let the life of Frederick Douglass be an example to those who must take up the conflict where he was obliged to lay it down, and a warning to those who would put aside and cover up the wrongs done to-day, in the name of science and of that new God which measures human rights, not by manhood but by race and color, making the shallow claim of a supreme superiority the excuse for wrong. A nation, a civilization, a Christianity, which within one man's memory upheld slavery with all its horrors should hesitate to proclaim anew its infallibility. The land which gave a million lives to destroy the demon Slavery, should beware of enthroning in its place the fouler and more dangerous Moloch, Caste!

As slave, freedman, citizen, and patriot, Frederick Douglass' life was such as to reflect fame upon his people, credit upon those who listened to his admonitions, renown upon the nation, which finally recognized his merits, and honor on all who do honor to his memory. Within this fane dedicated to liberty and the memory of noble sons of the Republic, no worthier life has been commemorated.

PAUL LAURENCE DUNBAR [8]

A hush is over all the teeming lists,
  And there is pause, a breath-space in the strife;
A spirit brave has passed beyond the mists
  And vapors that obscure the sun of life.
And Ethiopia, with bosom torn,
Laments the passing of her noblest born.

She weeps for him a mother's burning tears—
  She loved him with a mother's deepest love.
He was her champion thro' direful years,
  And held her weal all other ends above.
When Bondage held her bleeding in the dust,
He raised her up and whispered, "Hope and Trust."

For her his voice, a fearless clarion, rung
  That broke in warning on the ears of men;
For her the strong bow of his power he strung,
  And sent his arrows to the very den
Where grim Oppression held his bloody place
And gloated o'er the mis'ries of a race.

And he was no soft-tongued apologist;
  He spoke straightforward, fearlessly uncowed;
The sunlight of his truth dispelled the mist,
  And set in bold relief each dark-hued cloud;
To sin and crime he gave their proper hue,
And hurled at evil what was evil's due.

Through good and ill report he cleaved his way
  Right onward, with his face set toward the heights,
Nor feared to face the foeman's dread array,—
  The lash of scorn, the sting of petty spites.
He dared the lightning in the lightning's track,
And answered thunder with his thunder back.

The place and cause that first aroused his might
  Still proved its power until his latest day.
In Freedom's lists and for the aid of Right
  Still in the foremost rank he waged the fray;

[8] Paul Laurence Dunbar, "Frederick Douglass," in *Lyrics of Lowly Life* (New York: Dodd, Mead & Co., 1897), pp. 8–11.

Wrong lived; his occupation was not gone.
He died in action with his armor on!

We weep for him, but we have touched his hand,
 And felt the magic of his presence nigh,
The current that he sent throughout the land,
 The kindling spirit of his battle-cry.
O'er all that holds us we shall triumph yet,
And place our banner where his hopes were set!

Oh, Douglass, thou hast passed beyond the shore,
 But still thy voice is ringing o'er the gale!
Thou'st taught thy race how high her hopes may soar,
 And bade her seek the heights, nor faint, nor fail.
She will not fail, she heeds thy stirring cry,
She knows thy guardian spirit will be nigh,
And, rising from beneath the chast'ning rod,
She stretches out her bleeding hands to God!

DOUGLASS IN HISTORY

19

Kelly Miller: Douglass and Washington[1]

In the year that Douglass died Booker T. Washington made a speech in Atlanta, Georgia, which was essentially a plea for understanding and good will between whites and Negroes. The speech was acclaimed throughout the country, and within five years Washington had become the most influential Negro in the country, a position he held until his death in 1915. Inevitably he was compared to Douglass, as in the following selection by Kelly Miller (writing under the pseudonym "Fair Play"). Miller, whose academic career was spent at Howard University as professor and dean in the liberal arts college, wrote extensively on Negro affairs, his essays appearing in well known magazines. His style was vigorous, although marked by the objectivity of one who sees things from many angles and who thus inclines to take the middle road.

When a distinguished Russian was informed that some American Negroes were radical and some conservative, he could not restrain his laughter. The idea of conservative Negroes was more than the Cossack's risibilities could endure. "What on earth," he exclaimed with astonishment, "have they to conserve?"

According to a strict construction of terms, a conservative is one

[1] From Kelly Miller, "Boston Transcript," in *The Colored American Magazine* (Boston), November, 1903, pp. 824–26.

who is satisfied with, and advocates the continuance of, existing conditions; while a radical clamors for amelioration through change. No thoughtful Negro is satisfied with the present status of his race, whether viewed in its political, civil or general aspect. He labors under an unfriendly public opinion which is being rapidly crystallized into rigid caste and enacted into unrighteous law. How can he be expected to contemplate such oppressive conditions with satisfaction and composure? Circumstances render it imperative that his attitude should be dissentient rather than conformatory. Every consideration of enlightened self-respect impels to unremitting protest, albeit the manner of protestation may be mild or pronounced, according to the dictates of prudence. Radical and conservative Negroes agree as to the end in view, but differ as to the most effective means of attaining it. The difference is not essentially one of principle or purpose, but point of view. All anti-slavery advocates desired the downfall of the iniquitous institution, but some were more violent than others in the expression of this desire. Disagreement as to method led to personal estrangement, impugnment of motive, and unseemly factional wrangle. And so, colored men who are zealous alike for the betterment of their race, lose half their strength in internal strife, because of variant methods of attack upon the citadel of prejudice. The recent regrettable "Boston riot" [2] is a striking case in point. Mr. Booker T. Washington is the storm center about which the controversy rages. Contending forces have aligned themselves in hostile array, as to the wisdom or folly of the doctrine of which he is the chief exponent. Two recent occurrences have served to accentuate this antagonism.

1. About two yars ago, a group of Boston colored men, exotics, as some would say, of New England colleges, who had grown restive under the doctrine of the famous Tuskegeean, founded the "Boston Guardian" as a journal of protest. These men believe that the teachings of Mr. Washington are destructive of the rights and liberties of the race, and are pledged to spare no effort to combat what they deem his damaging doctrine. Mr. William Monroe Trotter, a Harvard graduate, and who is said to have maintained a higher scholastic average than any other colored student at that famous

[2] While speaking in Boston in July, 1903, Washington had been heckled by Negro militants. Things got out of hand, necessitating a call for the police.

institution, is head and front of the movement. Mr. Trotter possesses considerable independent means, and is as uncompromising as William Lloyd Garrison.

2. The recent publication of "The Souls of Black Folk," by Professor W. E. B. Du Bois, also a Harvard graduate, has added new emphasis to the prevailing controversy. Dr. Du Bois is not an agitator, nor a carping critic of another's achievements, but a scholar, a painstaking, accurate investigator, a writer of unusual lucidity and keenness, and a fearless advocate of the higher aspirations of his race. He has stated in pointed, incisive terms, the issue between Mr. Washington and his critics, and has given the controversy definiteness and cast. Du Bois and Washington are being held up to public view as contrasted types of Negro leadership.

The radical and conservative tendencies cannot be better described than by comparing, or rather contrasting, the two superlative colored men in whom we find their highest embodiment—Frederick Douglass and Booker Washington. The two men are in part products of their times, but are also natural antipodes. Douglass lived in the day of moral giants; Washington in the era of merchant princes. The contemporaries of Douglass emphasized the rights of man; those of Washington his productive capacity. The age of Douglass acknowledged the sanction of the Golden Rule; that of Washington worships the Rule of Gold. The equality of men was constantly dinned into Douglass's ears; Washington hears nothing but the inferiority of the Negro and the dominance of the Saxon. Douglass could hardly receive a hearing to-day; Washington would have been hooted off the stage a generation ago. Thus all truly useful men must be, in a measure, time-servers; for unless they serve their time, they can scarcely serve at all. But great as was the diversity of formative influences that shaped these two great lives, there is no less opposability in their innate bias of souls. Douglass was like a lion, bold and fearless; Washington is lamblike, meek and submissive. Douglass escaped from personal bondage, which his soul abhorred; but for Lincoln's proclamation, Washington would probably have arisen to esteem and favor in the eyes of his master as a good and faithful servant. Douglass insisted upon right; Washington upon duty. Douglass held up to public scorn the sins of the white man; Washington portrays the faults of his own race. Douglass spoke what he thought the world should hear; Washington only what he feels it is disposed to listen to. Douglass's conduct was actuated by principle; Washington's by prudence. Douglass had no limited, copyrighted program for his race, but appealed to the decalogue, the golden rule, the Declaration of Independence, the Constitution of the United States; Washington, holding these great principles in the shadowy background, presents a practical expedient applicable to present needs. Douglass was a moralist, insisting upon the application of righteousness to public affairs; Washington is a practical statesman, accepting the best terms which he thinks it possible to secure.

Washington came upon the stage at the time when the policies which Douglass embodied had seemed to fail. Reconstruction measures had proven abortive. Negro politicians, like Othello, had lost their occupations, and had sought asylum in the Government departments at Washington. The erstwhile advocates of the Negro's cause had grown indifferent or apologetic. The plain intent of the Constitution had been overborne in the South with the connivance of the North. The idea of lifting the Negro to the plane of equality with the white race, once so fondly cherished, found few remaining advocates. Mr. Washington sized up the situation with the certainty and celerity of a genius. He based his policy upon the ruins of the one that had been exploited. He avoided controverted issues, and moved, not along the line of least resistance, but of no resistance at all. He founded his creed upon construction rather than criticism. He urged his race to do the things possible rather than whine and pine over things prohibited. According to his philosophy, it is better to build even upon the shifting sands of expediency than not to build at all, because you cannot secure a granite foundation. He thus hoped to utilize whatever residue of good feeling there might be in the white race for the betterment of the Negro.

20

T. S. Standing:
Hero to Negro Nationalists[1]

To the Negroes of the twentieth century Douglass took on the proportions of a folk hero. In an article on Negro leadership, written in 1934, a University of Iowa sociologist took note of Douglass's high reputation among colored Americans who were either race-conscious or militant or both.

One of the most interesting recent developments among American Negroes has been the growth of a militant sentiment of racial solidarity and race pride. It is this movement which is here referred to as Negro nationalism. To date its overt expressions have been less obvious than is the case with other more widely recognized nationalistic movements, but its essential nature appears to be similar. Most Negro leaders have been more or less associated with this nationalistic trend. But, when a study of Negro leadership is made in terms of the various historic periods during which the race has been resident in America, striking differences are revealed in the types of persons coming into prominence.

The slave régime offered little opportunity for the emergence of an independent type of Negro leadership. Most of the very few Negroes who achieved prominence during the slavery period were free residents of the North who were active in the anti-slavery agitation. Frederick Douglass was the most aggressive and conspicuous of this group. Yet, in spite of his militancy, Douglass can scarcely be characterized as a Negro nationalist. He was primarily an abolitionist and, as such, his appeal was not so much to his own racial group

[1] From T. S. Standing, "Nationalism in Negro Leadership," *American Journal of Sociology,* XL (September, 1934), 180–81. Reprinted by permission of The University of Chicago Press.

as to the white society which he hoped to influence. He did not, as some of his more recent and radical successors, preach a gospel of racial self-sufficiency and anti-Nordicism.

The importance of Frederick Douglass to the nationalistic movement lies in the fact that since his death he has come to be regarded as a racial hero. He has become one of the most prominent figures in a growing list of Negro patriots, and his picture, along with that of Booker Washington, is displayed in countless Negro homes and schoolrooms.

Aside from Douglass, there were few Negro leaders of any consequence prior to the Civil War. A few preachers of the period attained some local reputation, but they were for the most part ignorant persons, and their message one of emotional exhortation in the practice of the Christian virtues of meekness and resignation. There were a few slave insurrections during the pre-war period, but their leaders were also local characters remembered chiefly because of the advertising given them in the current abolitionist press.

The brief period of Negro enfranchisement following the Civil War brought into state offices a number of local Negro politicians and resulted in the election of a few more competent individuals to the national congress. Yet Frederick Douglass remained the only really outstanding colored man outside of the Negro clergy.

21

Philip S. Foner: Douglass in Marxian Perspective[1]

*It is but natural a militant like Douglass would at-
tract writers who were of a liberal outlook and, even more,
those who were committed to a revolutionary philosophy. The
Marxist-oriented historian, Philip S. Foner, viewed Douglass
as the personification of the struggle against evils inherent in
the American society of his day, a shining example of steadfast
resistance to oppression. Although Foner does give Douglass a
few bad marks, he places him in a class he reserves only for
Jefferson and Lincoln.*

Perhaps no one in our history with so little official position
ever achieved so much. He lived to see most of the demands he had
raised before, during, and immediately after the Civil War to establish and guarantee freedom for the Negro people become the law
of the land. Unfortunately, he also lived to see many of these laws,
particularly the Fourteenth and Fifteenth Amendments, become
dead-letters after the betrayal of the Negro people in the "peace
agreement" of 1876 and in the resulting victory of the former
Southern ruling class.

But Douglass did not retreat to his study to reminisce over the
battles and victories of the past. Once again he took to the lecture
platform to explain the issues and to raise the demand that the
nation enforce the democratic rights guaranteed to the Negro
people and now being denied to them. He had no patience with
the doctrine of gradualism. To those who insisted: "Be patient! We

[1] From Philip S. Foner, *Frederick Douglass* (New York: International Publishers Co., Inc., 1964), pp. 369–70, 371, 372, 374, 376. Reprinted by permission
of the publisher.

must move slowly. Remember, your people have made wonderful progress in your own lifetime; don't upset the apple cart"—he invariably replied: "We demand full equality now!" While he recognized that all the barriers against the Negro people could not be leveled overnight by executive fiat, court decisions, or legislative action, he was convinced that the battle for the achievement of full rights for the Negro American must be waged persistently and consistently.

We have spoken of certain shortcomings of Douglass' leadership in his declining years. Douglass did not wage a sufficiently effective struggle for the economic guarantees of Negro freedom; he did not ally himself sufficiently with the emerging labor movement; he did not do enough to mobilize opposition to the Republican party's betrayal of the Negro freedmen and of democracy. At a time when Douglass was still clinging to the Republican party, significant sections of the Negro population, disillusioned with that party because of its failure to live up to its promises, were allying themselves with independent labor and farmer parties as a means of winning full political rights and bettering their economic conditions. But Douglass, still tied to the Republican party, remained aloof from the alliance between sections of the Negro population and the independent political movements of workers and farmers.

In truth, Douglass failed to understand that the big-business interests which dominated the Republican party had long since receded from their advanced position during the early stages of Reconstruction when they had championed Negro civil and political rights in order to consolidate the triumph of Northern capitalism over the former slavemasters. He did not understand that when the bourgeois power had been consolidated and the conditions established for the rapid evolution of trusts and monopolies, the big-business interests which dominated the Republican party would, in alliance with the Bourbon elements in the South, become the chief obstacle in the path of Negro liberation.

All this, while true, cannot obscure the fact that at all times, Douglass stood squarely and uncompromisingly for the full freedom of the Negro people. Nor can it obscure the fact that at a time when some Negro leaders were advocating conciliation and compromise, not to say surrender, Douglass uncompromisingly adhered to his principles of unflinching opposition to the entire pattern of segregation.

In his phenomenal rise above some of the restrictions of the American caste system, Douglass consistently fought for those who were trapped in its tentacles. He bitterly denounced the unjust and brutal treatment of the mass of his people. Never fearing whom it might offend, he unflinchingly raised the cry for equality. . . .

In the early days of 1895, a young Negro student living in New England journeyed to Providence, Rhode Island, to seek the advice of the aged Frederick Douglass who was visiting that city. As their interview drew to a close the youth said, " 'Mr. Douglass, you have lived in both the old and the new dispensations. What have you to say to a young Negro just starting out? What should he do?' The patriarch lifted his head and replied, 'Agitate! Agitate! Agitate!' " . . .

But the spirit of fearless challenge which characterized the pioneer leader in the battle for Negro liberation did not perish. Negro men like Lewis H. Douglass, the departed leader's son, who fought against American imperialism, and Negro women like the remarkable Ida B. Wells, who fought the crime of lynching despite every attempt to silence her, and like Mrs. Mary Church Terrell and Mrs. Josephine S. Yates, who helped to form the National Association of Colored Women in 1896, continued to uphold the principles of Frederick Douglass by their militant resistance to oppression. . . .

Today Frederick Douglass still points the way. His struggle against all forms of discrimination, his exposure of the peonage system in the South, his campaign against lynching, and his demand that the Constitution be enforced, are as timely and significant today as they were in Douglass' lifetime. For Douglass' militant principles, carried out logically and translated into terms of today's problems, lead to the immediate outlawry of Jim-Crowism and all other manifestations of bigotry, to the passage and enforcement of anti-lynching legislation, to the removal of all barriers on the full exercise of the right of suffrage, and greater Negro representation in both elective and appointive offices, to the abolition of inequalities in education, to the elimination of the ghetto and restrictive covenants, to the abolition of discrimination in employment and the extirpation of every vestige of peonage, to common action between white and Negro Americans for an end to Negro oppression and for the removal of the stumbling blocks which stand in the way of full economic, political and social equality for the Negro people and progress and freedom for the entire nation. . . .

Not only a great Negro and passionate fighter against every injustice heaped upon his people, but a far-sighted statesman enlisted in the "cause of humanity the world over," and one who saw his people's liberation movement as part of the democratic advance of all Americans, Frederick Douglass has grown in stature and significance since his death. "It is 58 years since Frederick Douglass, that most illustrious Negro and to my mind the greatest of all Americans died . . . ," wrote Mrs. Mary Church Terrell in the September, 1953, issue of *Ebony* Magazine. "The passing of the years, far from diminishing his importance, has made Douglass an even greater figure in his country's history." His memory and his heritage will not die, for he takes his deserved place with Jefferson and Lincoln in the democratic tradition of our country.

22

August Meier: Blueprint
for Black People[1]

*August Meier, professor of history at Kent State
University, a highly acclaimed scholar in the field of historical
studies on the Negro and a leading authority on the civil rights
movements of the twentieth century, has systematically analyzed Douglass's ideologies relating to the advancement of
Negroes. In an article entitled, "Frederick Douglass' Vision for
America: A Case Study in Nineteenth Century Negro Protest,"
Meier discusses the programs Douglass advocated for full
equality, and the relationship of those programs to the dominant patterns in nineteenth century Negro thought.*

The most distinguished Negro in nineteenth century America
was Frederick Douglass. His fame rests chiefly upon his work as a
brilliant anti-slavery orator and newspaper editor. Yet Douglass was
also deeply concerned with developing a program to secure full
citizenship rights and acceptance in American society for the free
Negroes—both for the minority who were free before the Civil War
and for the great masses after emancipation. With his thinking
rooted in the principles of American democracy and Christianity—
in the Declaration of Independence and the Sermon on the Mount
—Douglass' life was a moral crusade for the abolition of slavery
and racial distinction, the attainment of civil and political rights
and equality before the law, and the assimilation of Negroes into
American society. However his specific tactics and programs for

[1] From August Meier, "Frederick Douglass' Vision for America: A Case Study
in Nineteenth Century Negro Protest," in *Freedom and Reform: Essays in Honor
of Henry Steele Commager,* eds. Harold M. Hyman and Leonard W. Levy (New
York: Harper & Row, Publishers, 1967). Reprinted without the footnotes by permission of the editors, author, and publisher.

racial elevation might vary—and they did undergo significant changes over the years—Douglass was ever the militant agitator, ever the forthright editor and orator, who consistently worked toward these goals through his half century (1841–1895) of leadership.

Douglass' anti-slavery career has received detailed treatment at the hands of other scholars, but his ideologies concerning the advancement of free Negroes have not yet been the subject of systematic analysis. This paper therefore is limited to a discussion of the programs he advocated for the achievement of full racial equality, and the relationship of these programs to the dominant patterns in nineteenth century Negro thought.

Today, in the mid-twentieth century, Negro protest is expressed in the form of demands rather than appeals, in terms of power as well as justice, and is identified with a strategy of "direct action" rather than one of oratory and propaganda. The character of modern Negro protest is bottomed on the international pressures raised in behalf of American Negroes, the growing support for civil rights in the white population, and the increasing power of the Negro vote, which now acts as a balance of power in national elections. Throughout the nineteenth century, however, Negroes lacked leverage of this sort. Accordingly they utilized the written and spoken word as their major vehicle of protest, combining denunciation of the undemocratic and unchristian oppression under which they lived, with pleas directed at awakening the conscience of white Americans in order to secure redress of these grievances and recognition of their constitutional rights. Instances of what we would today call direct action did occur, but they were rare. Where conditions warranted it—as in those states where the antebellum Negroes could vote, and especially during Reconstruction—advocacy of political activity, in itself the central constitutional right which Negroes asked, was a leading theme, supplementing and lending weight to written and oral agitation, to conventions and meetings, to petitions and resolutions.

On the other hand articulate Negroes in that era ordinarily gave nearly equal emphasis to urging Negroes to cultivate good character, to be thrifty and industrious, and to acquire as much property as possible. It was believed that by thus achieving middle-class moral and economic respectability, Negroes would earn the respect of the whites, counteract prejudice, and ease the way toward recognition of their manhood and their citizenship.

Many nineteenth century advocates of thrift, industry, and economic accumulation placed special emphasis on the value of industrial education or training in mechanical trades. Most prominently associated with the accommodating ideology of Booker T. Washington at the end of the century, industrial education had been seriously advocated by prominent Negroes as early as the 1830's. Many Negro and white abolitionists viewed manual labor schools, where the students earned their way through the productive work they performed while learning a useful trade, as an instrument for uplifting the lowly of both races and assimilating them into the mainstream of American middle-class society. Such schools, it was believed, would inculcate the values of thrift and industry at the same time that they provided the students with the means of making a living. At mid-century, the economic crisis facing unskilled Negro workers, fostered a resurgence of interest in industrial training.

Underlying the moral and economic program was a theme of individual and racial self-help that in turn overlapped with an ideology of racial solidarity—of racial cooperation and racial unity. This ideology of racial solidarity was one that caused considerable division and argument among articulate nineteenth century Negroes. While a few went so far as to question the advisability of Negro churches and social organizations, the debate raged chiefly over whether or not Negroes should form their own protest organizations, and establish and support their own protest publications, rather than rely solely upon cooperation with sympathetic whites. This division of opinion was due to more than the attitudes and policies of the many white abolitionists who failed to concern themselves with the Negroes' citizenship rights, who objected to employing Negroes in other than menial positions, and who even refused to allow Negroes to participate fully in the decision-making process of the anti-slavery societies. It was more than an argument over the question of whether or not it was consistent for Negroes to ask for integration and for acceptance into the mainstream of white society, and at the same time segregate themselves into separate organizations. Beyond these matters the debate was rooted in a fundamental ethnic dualism—an identification with both American society on the one hand, and the persecuted Negro group on the other. This dualism arose out of the contradiction in American culture as Negroes experienced it: the contradiction between the American dream of equality for all and the reality of American race prejudice and discrimination.

Racial solidarity and self-help were always most characteristically associated with the advocacy of morality and economic accumulation, and like these doctrines tended to be especially popular in periods of greatest discouragement, particularly during the 1850's and again at the end of the century. During the decade before the Civil War, the passage of the Fugitive Slave Law of 1850, the decline of the anti-slavery societies, the increasing competition for menial and laboring jobs offered by Irish immigrants, the southern ascendancy in the national government which culminated in the Dred Scott decision, all made the outlook appear increasingly hopeless. Later, after the overthrow of Reconstruction, the increasing disfranchisement, segregation and mob violence in the South and, by the 1890's, the growing evidence of prejudice and discrimination in the North, again "forced the Negro back upon himself," as contemporaries expressed it. In the latter period protest efforts declined sharply, and the advocacy of racial solidarity, self-help, and economic and moral uplift tended to be most often coupled with an ideology of accommodation, especially in the South. This combination of ideas received its most notable expression in the philosophy of Booker T. Washington.

Proposals for racial union, self-help and solidarity, are generally recognized as a variety of Negro "nationalism." It was a form of nationalism which insisted upon the Negro's American citizenship, and viewed the cultivation of race pride and unity as a prerequisite for Negroes organizing themselves for the struggle to obtain equality and integration in American society. Related to this kind of ideology, though eschewing the ethnic dualism and the notion that Negroes could ever hope to achieve freedom and equal rights in the United States, was the philosophy of emigration or colonization. Its advocates held that the only solution to the problems facing American Negroes was to emigrate and create a national state of their own, either in the Caribbean area or in Africa. Such proposals, especially popular during the 1850's, cropped up with varying intensity throughout the century. Actually the function of colonization as an ideology was ambiguous. While its advocates protested vigorously against race discrimination in America, they nevertheless favored a form of withdrawal that was in effect an escapist accommodation to the American race system, rather than an assault upon it.

Except for colonization Douglass enunciated all of these ideologies—agitation, political action, the practice of morality and economy and the acquisition of property, self-help and racial cooperation. Like other Negroes he shifted his emphasis as the changing situation seemed to warrant. Yet Douglass' views are not simply a reflection of what Negroes generally were saying. Ever the independent thinker he was willing at times to diverge widely from the patterns of thought ascendant among his friends and contemporaries.

I. The Ante-Bellum Era

While in the latter part of the century Douglass was a symbol rather than a man of broad influence, during the years prior to the Civil War he was undoubtedly the most powerful leader in the northern Negro community, and his views roughly paralleled the ascendant ideologies among the ante-bellum free people of color.

Because there was an interrelationship between his program for securing the emancipation of the slaves and his proposals for advancing the status of free Negroes, a brief recapitulation of his anti-slavery career is in order. Born a slave on the Eastern shore of Maryland, Douglass succeeded in escaping from his Baltimore master in 1838. By 1841 he had entered the ranks of Massachusetts abolitionist orators. His public career during the abolitionist period may be fairly neatly divided into two parts: the 1840's when he followed the moral suasion tactics of the Garrisonians, and the 1850's when he espoused the cause of political abolition. The four years following the establishment of his weekly newspaper, *North Star,* in Rochester, were a period of transition during which, influenced by western abolitionists like Gerrit Smith, he re-examined his views and finally came to support political abolition, openly breaking with Garrison in 1851. From then on, agitation for political rights and stress upon the value of political activity became one of the most important themes in his thinking, and one which he articulated consistently for the rest of his life. Moreover it was probably from his abolitionist role that Douglass derived a belief in the value of verbal agitation, and a social philosophy which saw the world in essentially moral terms, explaining social institutions and social change as based on the good and evil propensities in human nature. To Douglass the solution of America's race problem lay not in any fundamental institutional changes, beyond the destruction of slavery. Rather the solution lay in a sincere effort to apply the moral principles upon which the Republic was founded. How to activate these moral principles was his major life-long concern.

In the years from the founding of *North Star* to the election of Lincoln, Douglass' program for the advancement of free Negroes consisted of three principal elements: a major emphasis on protest and citizenship rights, and secondary emphases on self-help, race pride and racial solidarity on the one hand, and economic development on the other. First and foremost he regarded Negroes as Americans:

> By birth, we are American citizens; by the principles of the Declaration of Independence, we are American citizens; within the meaning of the United States Constitution, we are American citizens; by the facts of history . . . by the hardships and trials endured, by the courage and fidelity displayed by our ancestors in defending the liberties and in achieving the independence of our land, we are American citizens.

Only on the rarest of occasions did his alienation and anger lead him to declare that "I have no love for America," and that he could feel no patriotism for a country like the United States, or to warn that the oppressed black men might some day rise up and "become the instruments of spreading desolation, devastation, and death throughout our borders."

Douglass constantly condemned the prejudice and discrimination which Negroes met daily: the segregation; the lack of economic opportunity; the exclusion from churches and schools, from juries and armed forces; and above all the disfranchisement. He denounced the "shameful" and "diabolical" Black Laws of Ohio as "the servile work of pandering politicians." He called upon the white people of Ohio to repeal the Black Laws and enfranchise the Negro, thus wiping out "a most foul imputation" upon their character and making Ohio "the paragon of all the free states." In 1860, in the midst of a campaign to abolish the discriminatory franchise qualifications of the New York State Constitution, he declared:

> It is a mockery to talk about protection in a government like ours to a class in it denied the elective franchise. The very denial of that right strips them of "protection," and leaves them at the mercy of all that is low, vulgar, cruel and base in the community, The ballot box and the jury box both stand closed against the man of color. . . . The white people of this country would wade knee deep in blood before they would be deprived of either of these means of protection against power and oppression.

Not satisfied with more resolves and declarations, Douglass was constantly in active rebellion against segregation and discrimination in all its forms, and was one of the few men of his time who engaged in what today would be regarded as nonviolent direct action. While residing in Massachusetts in the early 1840's he refused to ride on the Jim Crow railroad car, and was forcibly removed from the white coach. He withdrew his daughter from school rather than permit her to attend segregated schools in Rochester, and agitated for their elimination until he was successful. As one of his biographers says, "He made it a point to go into hotels, sit down at tables in restaurants, and enter public carriers." A well-known incident was his insistence upon being admitted to the reception President Lincoln held on the eve of his second inauguration, even though the guards tried to keep him out.

Douglass was interested in more than protesting against discrimination and agitating for citizenship rights. Firmly in the American middle-class tradition he also campaigned for "education, that grand lever of improvement," and for moral elevation and economic independence. While "not insensible" to the "withering prejudice" and "malignant and active hate" that placed obstacles in the Negro's pathway to respectability "even in the best parts of the country," he nevertheless believed "The fact that we are limited and circumscribed, ought rather to incite us to a more vigorous and persevering

use of the elevating means within our reach, than to dishearten us."
What Negroes needed, he went on, was character, and this they
could only obtain for themselves through hard toil. "A change in
our political condition would do very little for us without this. . . .
Industry, sobriety, honesty, combined with intelligence and a due
self-respect, find them where you will, among black or white, *must
be looked up to*." With character would come power, in the sense
that with it "we may appeal to the sense of justice alive in the
public mind, and by an honest, upright life, we may at least wring
from a reluctant public the all-important confession that we are
men, worthy men, good citizens, good Christians, and ought to be
treated as such." True, hostility was directed not at the lower class
Negroes whom whites found acceptable in their subordinate status,
but against respectable Negroes; but this, he asserted, was only
because color had for so long been associated in the public mind
with the degradation of slavery. If Negroes generally acquired
middle-class ways, whites would cease to couple undesirable qualities
with a black skin.

Along with this emphasis on Negroes helping themselves through
moral elevation and the cultivation of good character, went a decided interest in economic matters—an interest greatly intensified
by the growing competition from immigrants who threatened the
Negroes' hold upon even the unskilled and service occupations.
Accordingly Douglass emphatically urged the acquisition of skilled
trades to stave off impending disaster. Dramatically he called upon
Negroes to "Learn Trades or Starve." In phraseology that was
remarkably similar to that which Washington employed a half
century later Douglass insisted:

> We must become valuable to society in other departments of indus-
> try than those service ones from which we are rapidly being excluded.
> We must show that we can *do* as well as *be;* and to this end we must
> learn trades. When we can build as well as live in houses; when we
> can *make* as well as *wear* shoes; when we can produce as well as con-
> sume *wheat,* corn and rye—then we shall become valuable to society.
> Society is a hard-hearted affair. With it the helpless may expect no
> higher dignity than that of paupers. The individual must lay society
> under obligation to him, or society will harbor him only as a

stranger. . . . *How* shall this be done? In this manner: Use every means, strain every nerve to master some important mechanic art.

Neither classical education, nor "holding conventions and passing strong resolutions" could prevent the "degradation of Negroes. . . . The fact is . . . the education of the hand must precede that of the head. We can never have an educated class until we have more men of means amongst us." Negroes could not become merchants or professional men "in a single leap," but only "when we have patiently and laboriously . . . passed through the intermediate gradations of agriculture and mechanic arts." Backed by an offer of financial assistance (later withdrawn) from Harriet Beecher Stowe, Douglass presented a proposal for a manual labor school to the National Convention of Negro leaders which met at Rochester in 1853. The conferees, convinced that a strong emphasis on racial solidarity and economic accumulation was essential to the securing of citizenship rights, enthusiastically endorsed Douglass' plan.

The hopes of the Rochester Convention proved illusory. Nevertheless it is significant that over a generation before industrial education became a major plank in Booker T. Washington's platform of accommodation, arguments almost identical to those later employed by the Tuskegeean had been utilized by the noted protest leader, Frederick Douglass, to justify emphasis on training for the trades over education for the learned professions.

For Douglass, of course, the advocacy of character development and economic accumulation was no substitute for agitation for citizenship rights. When Horace Greeley in 1855 urged Negroes to stop agitating for the vote and instead direct their energies toward achieving the economic standing necessary for them to meet the discriminatory franchise qualifications of New York State, Douglass replied:

> Why should *we* be told to break up our Conventions, cease "jaw-ing" and "clamoring," when others equally *"indolent, improvident, servile and licentious"* (all of which adjectives we reject as untruthful . . .) are suffered to indulge . . . in similar demonstrations? In a word, why should we be sent to hoeing, and planting corn, to digging potatoes, and raising cabbages, as the *"preferable and more*

effective" method of abrogating the unjust, anti-Republican and disgraceful race restrictions imposed upon us, in the property qualification?

Thus for Douglass the acquisition of morality and property was a supplemental instrument in the struggle for equal rights. Character and wealth certainly did not take precedence over protest and agitation, or an appeal to the conscience of white America, based upon its democratic and egalitarian values.

Deteriorating conditions also led Douglass to place considerable emphasis on self-help and racial solidarity. The *North Star* in fact was founded in a period when the advocacy both of these ideas and of colonization was on the rise. In fact in the very first issue Douglass urged his "oppressed countrymen" to "remember that we are one, that our cause is one, and that we must help each other, if we would succeed. . . . We are indissolubly united, and must fall or flourish together." He criticized Negroes for depending too much on whites to better their condition. True, he counselled Negroes to "Never refuse to act with a white society or institution because it is white, or a black one, because it is black. But act with all men without distinction of color. . . . We say avail yourselves of *white* institutions, not because they are white, but because they afford a more convenient means of improvement." Nevertheless he maintained that "the main work must be commenced, carried on, and concluded by ourselves . . . our destiny, for good or evil . . . is, by an all-wise God, committed to us. . . . It is evident that we can be improved and elevated only just so fast and far as we shall improve and elevate ourselves."

Douglass perceived that race prejudice produced among Negroes what in today's terms would be called an awareness of a separate identity. He held that while all men were brothers, and were "naturally and self-evidently entitled to all the rights, privileges and immunities common to every member of that family," nevertheless "the force of potent circumstance" made it proper for him to address Negroes as "our own people." Indeed he referred to Negroes as an oppressed "nation within a nation," slave and free alike united in a "destiny [that] seems one and the same." He proposed a "Union of the Oppressed for the Sake of Freedom," to organize Negroes in order to obtain their rights and elevate themselves through collective effort. His propaganda bore fruit when the Rochester Convention of 1853, which marked the high tide of enthusiasm for racial solidarity among the ante-bellum Negro conventions, organized an abortive Protective Union to coordinate race interests and efforts.

Douglass defended his plans for racial union against charges that such a segregated organization would create a "complexional issue." It was not the colored men, but whites who, by their policy of discrimination, had created a "complexional issue." As he put it in 1855, in roundly criticizing that class of abolitionists who kept Negroes subservient to whites in the movement:

> Every day brings with it renewed evidence of the truthfulness of the sentiment, now . . . gaining the confidence and sympathy of our oppressed People, THAT OUR ELEVATION AS A RACE, IS ALMOST WHOLLY DEPENDENT UPON OUR OWN EXERTIONS. . . . The history of other oppressed nations will confirm us in this assertion . . . the oppressed nation itself, has always taken a prominent part in the conflict.

Douglass, with his feeling that prejudice and discrimination made Negroes a "nation within a nation," resembled many other articulate Negroes of this period in exhibiting strong ethnocentric tendencies. Yet he never went as far as did a number of others who completely rejected American society and advocated colonization. It is not unlikely that a majority of Negro leaders at one time or another in the 1850's espoused emigration, but Douglass consistently affirmed that

> Nothing seems more evident to us, than that our destiny is sealed up with that of the white people of this country, and we believe that we must fall or flourish with them. We must banish all thought of emigration from our minds, and resolve to stay just where we are . . . among white people, and avail ourselves of the civilization of America.

Born in America, Negroes had fought and bled for the country: "we are here; . . . this is *our* country; . . . The white man's happiness cannot be purchased by the black man's misery. . . ." Even during the fifties, when colonization sentiments were making strong inroads into the thinking of articulate Negroes, he opposed them. Writing to Henry Highland Garnet, the eminent Presbyterian minister and abolitionist who had become an emigrationist, Douglass maintained that the emigrationists actually weakened the efforts to elevate Negroes in this country, since they channeled their energies, which might have helped Negroes in the United States, into visionary colonization schemes.

Yet the pressure for expatriation was exceedingly strong. As the fifties drew to a close conditions seemed to grow worse. Lincoln's policy after his inauguration appeared to Douglass to be one of appeasing the slaveholders, and he was bitterly disappointed. Discouraged, he finally lent an open ear and eye toward emigration, and agreed to undertake a trip to Haiti; not with the intention of settling there himself, but to obtain information that might be useful to those who, alarmed at the persecution and hardships that were becoming "more and more rigorous and grievous with every year," were "looking out into the world for a place of retreat," and were "already resolved to look for homes beyond the boundaries of the United States."

Even before this editorial appeared in print the attack on Fort Sumter occurred. To Douglass this was a welcome event, and one which completely changed his plans. To him the war presaged both the emancipation of the slaves and the attainment of racial equality. As he said in a speech in Philadelphia in 1863, "The Mission of the War" was two fold: "the utter extirpation of slavery from every facet of American soil, and the complete enfranchisement of the entire colored people of this country."

II. Reconstruction and After

Douglass' war-time efforts to secure the emancipation of the slaves, and the admission of Negro soldiers to the Union armies, have been amply described by other scholars. Both of these activities were, in his view, but a prelude to the larger task of securing full citizenship rights and ending all forms of race discrimination. Speaking at the thirtieth anniversary meeting of the American Anti-Slavery Society in December, 1863, Douglass warned that the struggle was not over; "that our work will not be done until the colored man is admitted a full member in good and regular standing in the American body politic." Merely to abolish slavery was no solution to the race problem. Rather, "the question is: Can the white and colored peoples of this country be blended into a common nationality . . . and enjoy together in the same country, under the same flag, the inestimable blessings of life, liberty, and the pursuit of happiness, as neighborly citizens of a common country."

Over the course of the next two decades, during Reconstruction and the years immediately following, Douglass' philosophy retained the broad scope of the pre-Civil War decade, but with some differences in emphasis. Basically Douglass demanded the immediate and complete integration of Negroes into American society. He held to a vision of the United States as a "composite nation," in which all races of men participated without discrimination. "In whatever else other nations may have been great and grand," Douglass explained, "our greatness and grandeur will be found in the faithful application of the principle of perfect civil equality to the people of all races and creeds." Addressing the Massachusetts Anti-Slavery Society in the spring of 1865, he called for the " 'immediate, unconditional, and universal' enfranchisement of the black man." He pointed out that Negroes wanted the suffrage

> because it is our right, first of all. No class of men can, without insulting their own nature, be content with any deprivation of their rights. . . . Again, I want the elective franchise . . . because ours is a peculiar government, based upon a peculiar idea, and that idea is universal suffrage. If I were in a monarchical government, or an aristocratic government, where the few ruled and the many were subject, there would be no special stigma resting upon me because I did not exercise the elective franchise . . . . But here, where universal suffrage . . . is the fundamental idea of the Government, to rule us out is to make us an exception, to brand us with the stigma of inferiority, and to invite to our heads the missiles of those above us.

Later, when men hitherto friendly toward the Negroes, became critical of their stress on political rights, alleging that their interest in politics was "far more lively than is consistent" with their welfare, he conceded that no intelligent person could want to see the

Negroes "look to politics as their proper vocation, or to government as their only means of advancement." But he also insisted that "scarcely less deplorable would be the condition of this people, if among them there should be found no disposition . . . for political activity. That men who would advise the black man to make no effort to distinguish himself in politics, will advise him to omit one of the most important levers that can be employed to elevate his race."

Meanwhile Douglass placed greater emphasis on the gospel of wealth and racial cooperation than did most of his articulate contemporaries, though these ideas were less prominent in his ideology than formerly. As president of national conventions held by Negro leaders at Syracuse in 1864 and at Louisville in 1883 (Douglass presiding over both of them), he replied to critics of the idea of holding a race convention by calling attention to the prejudice and discrimination which Negroes still encountered, in spite of the Emancipation Proclamation and in spite of the legislation and constitutional amendments enacted during Reconstruction. When he and others established a newspaper known as *The New Era* in 1870, he appealed for Negro support for a race journal on the basis of self-help and racial solidarity: "Our friends," he declared, "can do much for us, but there are some things which colored men and women must do for themselves." Later he grew irate when Negroes failed to support the publication, and he criticized them because they were "not conscious of any associated existence or a common cause."

On economic matters his thoughts remained unchanged. In 1864 he advised the freedom "to shape their course toward frugality, the accumulation of property, and above all, to leave untried no amount of effort and self-denial to acquire knowledge, and to secure a vigorous moral and religious growth." Sixteen years later, in a rhetoric typical of the age, and in words that Booker T. Washington would have fully approved, he was uttering the standard pieties of middle-class Americans:

> Neither we, nor any other people, will ever be respected till we respect ourselves, and we will never respect ourselves till we have the means to live respectably. . . . A race which cannot save its

earnings, which spends all it makes . . . can never rise in the scale of civilization. . . .

   . . . This part of our destiny is in our own hands. . . . If the time shall ever come when we shall possess in the colored people of the United States, a class of men noted for enterprise, industry, economy and success, we shall no longer have any trouble in the matter of civil and political rights. The battle against popular prejudice will have been fought and won. . . . The laws which determine the destinies of individuals and nations are impartial and eternal. We shall reap as we shall sow. There is no escape. The conditions of success are universal and unchangeable. The nation or people which shall comply with them will rise, and those which violate them will fall.

Douglass' basically middle-class orientation towards the solution of the problems facing American Negroes is revealed in the way in which he expressed his very genuine concern with the problems of the Negro working classes. Basically he believed that the ordinary person, of whatever race, should strive to become an entrepreneur. He admitted that "the disproportionate distribution of wealth certainly is one of the evils which puzzle the greatest national economists," but thought that attacking capital was to attack a "symptom" rather than a cause. "Real pauperism," he continued, existed only in those states "where liberty and equality have been mere mockeries until lately." Workers had the right to strike, but Douglass thought it "tyranny" when they tried to prevent others from working in their places. Douglass' attitudes were perceptibly reinforced by a personal experience—the exclusion of his son from the typographical society of Washington. Yet on occasion he could express a vague consciousness of the identity of interest between white and black workers, as when he argued in 1883 that the white labor unions should not isolate themselves and "throw away this colored element of strength." Labor everywhere, regardless of race, wanted the same thing: "an honest day's pay for an honest day's work." Unity among black and white workers was desirable, he concluded, because "experience demonstrates that there may be a slavery of wages only a little less galling and crushing in its effects than chattel slavery, and this slavery of wages must go down with the other."

After the failure of Radical Reconstruction and the restoration of white supremacy in the South, Douglass' philosophy did not change; if anything he became more vigorous in his denunciations of caste and oppression and proscription. Writing in the *North American Review* in 1881 he denounced the growing repression in the South in scathing terms:

> Of all the varieties of men who have suffered from this feeling [of race prejudice] the colored people of this country have endured most. . . . The workshop denies him work, and the inn denies him shelter; the ballot-box a fair vote, and the jury-box a fair trial. He has ceased to be the slave of an individual, but has in some sense become the slave of society. . . .

Ridiculing the inconsistencies of the color line, he pointed out that the Chinese were hated because they were industrious, the Negroes because they were thought to be lazy. Southerners thought the Negro so deficient in "intellect and . . . manhood, that he is but the echo of the designing white man," and yet so strong and clear-headed "that he cannot be persuaded by arguments or intimidated by threats, and that nothing but the shot-gun can restrain him from voting. . . . They shrink back in horror from contact with the Negro as a man and a gentleman, but like him very well as a barber, writer, coachman or cook." Two years later, when the Supreme Court declared the Civil Rights Act of 1875 unconstitutional, Douglass, speaking at an indignation meeting in Washington, called the decision a "shocking" sign of "moral weakness in high places," a "calamity" resulting from the "autocratic" powers of the court, that embarrassed the country before the world. If the Civil Rights Act was "a bill for social equality, so is the Declaration of Independence, which declares that all men have equal rights; so is the Sermon on the Mount, so is the Golden Rule . . . ; so is the Apostolic teaching that of one blood, God has made all nations . . . ; so is the Constitution. . . ." Douglass became so bitter that in 1884 he suggested that Negroes might resort to violence. Unfortunately the "safety valves" provided by American institutions for the peaceful expression and redress of grievances—free speech, a free press, the right of assembly, and the ballot box—did not exist in the South.

Only such institutions made violence, and insurrection, daggers and dynamite, unnecessary for an oppressed people; and he warned the South that ideas were weapons and that the black man was aware of the example set by revolutionists in European countries. Such statements were extremely rare in Douglass' speeches; that he made them at this juncture reveals the depth of his disillusionment and anger as he observed the worsening situation of southern Negroes.

Meanwhile Douglass had developed misgivings about the compromising course of the Republican Party in regard to protecting the rights of southern Negroes, even though Presidents Hayes, Garfield, Arthur and Harrison appointed him to political office. Sharply criticized for his supposed support of the Compromise of 1877, Douglass, at the Louisville Convention in 1883 felt it necessary to defend himself from charges of indifference to the compromise. He described himself as "an uneasy Republican," who had opposed Hayes' policy. He was quoted as saying that "Parties are made for men and not men for parties . . . follow no party blindly. If the Republican Party cannot stand a demand for justice and fair play it ought to go down. . . ." Six years later, in a widely circulated address delivered before the Bethel Literary and Historical Society of Washington, the most celebrated forum in the American Negro community, Douglass defended the favorable comments he had made about Cleveland in 1885, and argued that even though the Republican Party had recently returned to power in Washington, "past experience makes us doubtful" that anything would be done for Negro rights. To Douglass the question was purely a moral one: the Republican defeat in the Congressional elections of 1890, like Blaine's defeat in 1884, were due to the fact that the Party had deserted the Negro's cause. "The success of the Republican Party," he averred, "does not depend mainly upon its economic theories. . . . Its appeal is to the conscience of the Nation, and its success is to be sought and found in firm adhesion to the humane and progressive ideas of liberty and humanity which called it into being."

Douglass had travelled a long road indeed from 1872 when he had uttered his famous phrase, "The Republican Party is the deck, all else is the sea." Yet he never deserted the party, and during the eighties campaigned vigorously on its behalf. "I am sometimes reproached," he once wrote, "[for] being too much addicted to the

Republican Party. I am not ashamed of that reproach." Negroes, he continued, owed a great deal to the Party, and to desert it would be to ignore both this debt and the atrocities suffered at the hands of southern Democrats. Indeed, in the final analysis the situation in the South, where the Democrats dominated, demanded loyalty to the Republicans, and at election time he expressed nothing but contempt for those Negroes who were Democrats—men whose talks were "rank with treason to the highest and best interest of the Negro race." Yet continued loyalty was not rewarded, and by 1892 Douglass confessed that he was lukewarm in his support of the Party.

III. The Final Decade

It is a noteworthy fact that during the 1880's and 1890's, as conditions grew worse, as Negro thought veered from emphasis on political activity and attainment of equal rights to doctrines of self-help, racial solidarity and economic advancement, Douglass' thought moved in an opposite direction to a position more consistently assimilationist than at any time since the founding of *North Star* in 1847. More than ever he stressed assimilation and amalgamation as the solution to the race problem, and he constantly asserted that it was not a Negro problem, to be solved largely by the Negro's efforts to acquire morality and wealth, but the problem of the nation and the whites who had created the situation. It should be stressed that these ideas were not new in Douglass' philosophy; what is notable is the shift in emphasis, for in the last years of his life he discarded almost completely the idea of self-help, ignored the theme of race solidarity, declaimed against race pride, and said little of the gospel of wealth.

One may surmise that this shift came about as a result of one or both of two factors. Undoubtedly he was deeply concerned about the rising ascendancy of an accommodating ideology which accepted white stereotypes of Negroes as ignorant, immoral, lazy and thriftless; blamed Negroes themselves for this state of affairs and for the white prejudice they suffered; placed the principal burden of Negro advancement upon Negroes themselves; accepted segregation; depreciated agitation and politics; and stressed self-help, character-building, the frugal virtues and the acquisition of wealth as a program for achieving the respect of the white man and thus, ultimately, it was implied, "earning" the "privilege" of enjoying citizenship rights. Accordingly Douglass may well have decided to cease stressing those aspects of his philosophy which had been appropriated by the accommodators.

More likely his ideological change was due largely to the influence of his second wife, a white woman, Helen Pitts, whom he married in January, 1884. Douglass had earlier expressed the view that race intermixture would increase, and the year preceding his second marriage he had declared: "There is but one destiny, it seems to me, left for us, and that is to make ourselves and be made by others a part of the American people in every sense of the word. Assimilation and not isolation is our true policy and our national destiny." The marriage caused quite an uproar among many Negroes, who accused Douglass of lacking race pride. As he wrote to his friend and supporter, George L. Ruffin: "What business has any man to trouble himself about the color of another man's wife? Does it not appear violently impertinent—this intermeddling? Every man ought to try to be content with the form and color of his own wife and stop at that." Two years later he explicitly predicted that amalgamation of the races would be the "inevitable" solution of the race problem.

In a widely reprinted address, originally delivered before the Bethel Literary Association in 1889, Douglass summarized the views he held during the last decade of his life. In the first place, he said, the problem was not one for Negroes to solve themselves: "It is not what we shall do but what the nation shall do and be, that is to settle this great national problem." Admittedly Negroes could in part combat hostility "by lives and acquirements which counteract and put to shame this narrow and malignant" prejudice. Indeed "we have errors of our own to abandon, habits to reform, manners to improve, ignorance to dispel, and character to build up."

Douglass then went on to specify, even though he ran "the risk of incurring displeasure," other errors committed by Negroes which contemporaries usually listed as virtues—race pride, race solidarity, and economic nationalism (or the advocacy of Negro support of Negro business). First among them was the "greater prominence of late" being given to the "stimulation of a sentiment we are pleased to call race pride," to which Negroes were "inclining most persistently and mischievously. . . . I find it in all our books, papers and speeches." Douglass could see nothing to be either proud or ashamed of in a "gift from the Almighty," and perceived "no benefit to be derived from this everlasting exhortation to the cultivation of race pride. On the contrary, I see in it a positive evil. It is building on a false foundation. Besides, what is the thing we are fighting against . . . but race pride . . . ? . . . Let us away with this supercilious nonsense."

A second error was the doctrine "that union among ourselves is an essential element of success in our relations with the white race." Douglass held that "our union is our weakness," that the trouble was that when assembled together "in numerous numbers" rather than scattered among whites, "we are apt to form communities by ourselves." This, in turn, "brings us into separate schools, separate churches, separate benevolent and literary societies, and the result is the adoption of a scale of manners, morals and customs peculiar to our condition . . . as an oppressed people." Moreover, "a nation within a nation is an anomaly. There can be but one American nation . . . and we are Americans." Negroes should yield as little as humanly possible to the circumstances that compelled them to maintain separate neighborhoods and institutions. "We cannot afford to draw the line in politics, trade, education, manner, religion, or civilization." Douglass then went on to ridicule as "another popular error flaunted in our faces at every turn, and for the most part by very weak and impossible editors," "the alleged duty of the colored man to patronize colored newspapers . . . because they happen to be edited and published by colored men." Though he continued to believe that an "able" Negro paper was "a powerful lever for the elevation and advancement of the race," colored journals like colored artisans should be supported only on the basis of the "character of the man and the quality of his work."

In short, during his last years, Douglass was the protest and assimilationist leader epitomized. Yet interestingly enough he was on friendly terms with Booker T. Washington. In 1892 he gave the Commencement Address at Tuskegee Institute, and two years later obtained a substantial gift for the school from an English friend. At the same time he proudly recalled his earlier advocacy of industrial education.

There is no reason to believe that Douglass would have favored Washington's ascendancy as a race leader, which began a few months after Douglass' death with Washington's famous address at the Atlanta Exposition in September 1895. It is true that during the 1850's, and even for some years after the Civil War, Douglass had frequently expressed himself in terms that were remarkably similar to those that Washington enunciated at the end of the century. Like Washington, and using the same arguments and clichés, Douglass had stressed the middle-class respectability; the importance of trades and industrial education; the necessity for self-help and racial solidarity. But unlike Washington, Douglass was always clear and explicit about his desire for full equality. In fact he always subordinated these aspects of his philosophy to his advocacy of agitation and political activity. He never employed the flattering and conciliatory phraseology of the Tuskegeean; he never put the principal blame on Negro shoulders, nor did he make Negro self-improvement a panacea for the solution of the race problem. Finally, unlike Washington, he never permitted his ends to be obscured by his emphasis on the means.

We have pointed out that as the constellation of ideas which Washington epitomized was achieving ascendancy in Negro thought during the years after Reconstruction, Douglass' writings and speeches moved in an opposite direction. Integration, assimilation, protest against segregation and all other forms of oppression, and spirited advocacy of political rights and political activity were the hallmarks of his creed. Washington's ascendancy symbolized Negro acquiescence in segregational disfranchisement and a soft-pedaling of political activity. And if there was one thing which Douglass had emphasized consistently from mid-century on it was the importance of political rights and political activity as essential for protecting Negroes and advancing their status in American society.

To raise Negroes to the highest status in American society, to secure their inclusion in the "body politic," to make them integrally a part of the American community, had been Douglass' aim, his vision, his dream. In constructing his program he naturally stressed and utilized the basic values and ideologies of American culture. If whites treasured political and civil rights, Negroes as a minority group treasured them even more. If white Americans valued self-help, independence, virtuous character, and the accumulation of property, these things would also be of inestimable aid to Negroes in their struggle for advancement. If white Americans were proud of their nationality and what they had achieved by the collective effort of the nation, Negroes also needed to be proud of themselves and cooperate with each other in order to advance and progress. Douglass, like his friends and associates, thus fashioned the basic ideologies of American civilization into a program for the elevation of a minority group that would secure its acceptance into the larger society. Beyond all else Douglass was the moralist, constantly appealing to the democratic and Christian values of brotherhood, equality and justice,—values which Americans cherished but which, for Negroes, remained unfulfilled. As Douglass put it in 1889: "The real question is whether American justice, American liberty, American civilization, American law and American Christianity can be made to include and protect alike and forever all American citizens. . . . It is whether this great nation shall conquer its prejudices, rise to the dignity of its professions and proceed in the sublime course of truth and liberty [which Providence] has marked out for it."

23

James M. McPherson: A Key to Our Times[1]

James M. McPherson views Douglass as a protest figure, whose viewpoints and actions furnish us with clues to a better assessment of the differing tactics employed by today's civil rights advocates, and one whose career therefore might add to a fuller understanding of an America currently at the crossroads in race relations. Professor McPherson, of the history department at Princeton University, has written extensively on the civil rights and reform movements of an earlier America, including two perceptive books, The Struggle for Equality *and* The Negro's Civil War.

Frederick Douglass was one of the most eminent Americans of the nineteenth century, and the story of his life could almost have been written by a black Horatio Alger. Born a slave on Maryland's Eastern Shore, Douglass knew privation as a child. One of his most vivid recollections of slavery was a constantly gnawing stomach: he was often "so pinched for hunger as to dispute with old 'Nep,' the dog, for the crumbs which fell from the kitchen table." His only clothing was a knee-length sackcloth shirt, and in the winter he had to crawl into a feed-bag and sleep in a closet to keep warm. For one year in his youth he was farmed out to a "slave breaker" who was widely known for his skill in beating obstreperous Negroes into cringing submissiveness. From such inauspicious beginnings Douglass rose to the heights of fame and power.

One of Douglass' most popular lectures was titled "Self-Made

[1] James M. McPherson, "Preface" to the Atheneum Edition of Benjamin Quarles, *Frederick Douglass* (New York: Atheneum Publishers, 1968), pp. v–xi. Copyright © 1968 by James M. McPherson. Reprinted by permission of Mr. McPherson and the publisher.

Men," whom he described as "men who, without the ordinary helps
of favoring circumstances, have attained knowledge, usefulness,
power, position, and fame in the world. They are the men who owe
nothing to birth, relationship, friendly surroundings, wealth inherited, or to early and approved means of education." Never inordinately modest, Douglass was in effect describing himself. With
an unknown father and a mother whom he rarely saw, he benefited
little from the "favoring circumstances" or "friendly surroundings"
of a family upbringing. Denied "early and approved means of education," he taught himself to read and write with only limited assistance from sympathetic whites. Owing nothing to birth, relationship,
or inherited wealth, he nevertheless achieved knowledge, usefulness,
position, and fame. Douglass was a prime example of an "inner-
directed" personality; he grew up subject to all the power of a
"peculiar institution" that crushed the spark and ambition of most
of its victims, yet somehow he found the inner resources to overcome the disadvantages of slavery. Early in life he conceived a desire
for freedom which burned and grew inside him until, after the
failure of one bold plan for escape, he finally struck out for the
North and freedom at the age of twenty-one. Douglass found the
North no paradise; the cruelties of race prejudice and Jim Crow
placed countless obstacles in his path, but these too he surmounted.

Even self-made men cannot go far without some help, however,
and Douglass received aid from members of both races. A white
woman taught him the alphabet and awakened the desires and
opportunities born of literacy. When he escaped from slavery in
Baltimore to freedom in New Bedford, Massachusetts, his path north-
ward was smoothed by the aid of friendly Negroes. In New Bedford
a white abolitionist shipbuilder offered Douglass a job as a calker,
but when the white calkers threatened to strike if Douglass was
hired, the escaped slave had to accept more menial employment. His
first regular job was in a whale-oil refinery owned by a Quaker
abolitionist. In 1841 Douglass, who had been reading the *Liberator*
for two years, made his first speech before whites at an anti-slavery
rally. Impressed by his simple but eloquent recital of the wrongs of
slavery personally experienced, the Massachusetts Anti-Slavery Society launched Douglass' career by signing him on as a paid lecturer.
In later years, when asked where he got his education, Douglass

replied: "From Massachusetts Abolition University, Mr. Garrison, president."

Douglass became an active participant in the anti-slavery politics of the 1850's, and was by turns a leader in the Liberty party, a Free Soiler, and a Republican. When war came in 1861, he bent every effort to make it an abolition war, and once this was achieved he helped to recruit Negro soldiers to fight for Union and freedom. When the war was over, Douglass' mission as an abolitionist was not ended. Along with other abolitionists and Radical Republicans he outspokenly advocated civil and political rights for the freedmen, for "I see little advantage in emancipation without this." The Republican party's Reconstruction policy, culminating in the Fourteenth and Fifteenth Amendments, made the Negro theoretically equal before the law. But practice fell short of theory, and Douglass spent much of the rest of his life unsuccessfully urging the government to make good on its commitment to equality.

Douglass never failed to protest vehemently against segregation, and often resisted attempts by railroad conductors, hotel clerks, and the like to deny him equal facilities. (He once held on to the seats in a railroad coach so tightly that it took several trainmen to eject him from the car, and the seats were torn loose along with Douglass.) When his children were denied admission to the white public schools in Rochester, Douglass led a movement that brought about desegregation of the schools. In 1895, according to a story that may be a apocryphal but nevertheless contains the essence of truth, a Negro student asked Douglass, then in the twilight of his career, what advice he had for a young man just starting out. Douglass replied without hesitation: "Agitate! Agitate! Agitate!"

Frederick Douglass' career is relevant to our own age. Douglass' insistence on "Freedom Now" has found its parallel in the civil rights movement of the 1960's. Eighty-five years ago Douglass asserted that agitation of the race problem would go on "until the public schools shall cease to be caste schools," "until the colored man's pathway to the ballot-box . . . shall be as smooth and as safe as the same is for the white citizen," "until the courts of the country shall grant the colored man a fair trial and a just verdict," "until color shall cease to be a bar to equal participation in the offices and honors of the country," "until the trades-unions, and the workshops of the country shall cease to proscribe the colored man," "until the American people shall make character, and not color, the criterion of respectability."

Douglass' life offers also a key to understanding the disillusionment with non-violence and the growing militance of the contemporary civil rights revolution. In his autobiography Douglass described the year he spent as a slave under Edward Covey, the famed "Negro breaker," as the low point of his life. Covey whipped him frequently in an effort to break Douglass' spirit, until one day the seventeen-year-old slave decided he had had enough. He turned on Covey and fought with him desperately for two hours, drawing blood from his oppressor and finally vanquishing him. After this encounter Covey was afraid of Douglass and never whipped him again. The whole experience was one of exhilaration and enlightenment for Douglass, "the turning-point in my life as a slave. It rekindled in my breast the smouldering embers of liberty . . . and revived a sense of my own manhood." Douglass had "reached the point at which I was *not afraid to die*. This spirit made me a freeman in *fact*, though I still remained a slave in *form*." He concluded that "the doctrine that submission to violence is the best cure for violence did not hold good as between slaves and overseers. He was whipped oftener who was whipped easiest." This psychological insight helps to explain the peculiar sense of exhilaration and release exhibited by urban Negro rioters in the 1960's. For them as for Douglass, retaliatory violence against the white man had a cleansing and lifting effect on the spirit, and seemed to bring about a psychological if not physical emancipation from the intolerable tensions of submission.

24
The Enduring Douglass

Alain Locke, art critic, author, editor, in 1925, of the volume, The New Negro, *which launched the Harlem Renaissance, and the first Negro American Rhodes Scholar, viewed Douglass as a man not to be measured by the yardstick of a single generation, "but of all times." In a Foreword, in 1940, to the Pathway Press edition of Douglass's* Life and Times, *Locke did not ignore the paradoxes and contradictions in his career. But what Locke saw chiefly in Douglass was his enduring appeal. This view that Douglass was a man to be remembered was expressed lyrically by Robert E. Hayden, whose literary reputation has been secure since the publication, in 1940, of his first volume of verse. A longtime member of the Fisk University faculty, his poetry awards include Grand Prize at the First World Festival of Negro Arts, held at Dakar, Senegal, in 1966.*

ALAIN LOCKE [1]

In the lengthening perspective of the Negro's history in America the career and character of Frederick Douglass take on more and more the stature and significance of the epical. For in terms of the race experience his was, beyond doubt, the symbolic career, typical, on the one hand, of the common lot, but on the other, inspiringly representative of outstanding achievement. Its basic pattern is that of the chattel slave become freeman, with the heroic accent, however, of self-emancipation and successful participation in the struggle for group freedom. Superimposed is the dramatic design of a personal history of achievement against odds, in the course of

[1] From Alain Locke, "Foreword," in Frederick Douglass, *Life and Times of Frederick Douglass* (New York: Pathway Press, 1941), pp. xv–xx. Reprinted by permission of Richard B. Moore, Pathway Press.

which the hero becomes both an acknowledged minority leader and spokesman and a general American publicist and statesman. Both chance and history conspired toward this, as he himself acknowledges, modestly enough, in his autobiography, but no one can come away from the reading of it except with the conviction that in mind and character he was, in large part, author of his own destiny. This heroic cast makes the story of Fred Douglass an imperishable part of the Negro epic, and should make his *Life and Times* . . . the classic of American Negro biography.

Another narrative of outstanding individual achievement and group service, however,—Booker Washington's *Up From Slavery,* has long held pre-eminence in popular attention and favor. Its author, himself a biographer of Frederick Douglass, gives an apt clue to at least one important reason for this,—a reason over and above the comparative inaccessibility of the Douglass *Life* to the general reading public. Washington speaks of the Douglass career as falling "almost wholly within the first period of the struggle in which the race problem has involved the people of this country,— the period of revolution and liberation." "That period is now closed," he goes on to say, "we are at present in the period of construction and readjustment." So different did it seem, then, to Washington in 1906 that he could regret "that many of the animosities engendered by the conflicts and controversies of half a century ago still survive to confuse the councils of those who are seeking to live in the present and future rather than in the past" and express the hope that nothing in Douglass's life narrative should "serve to revive or keep alive the bitterness of those controversies of which it gives the history." In so saying Washington does more than reveal the dominant philosophy of his own program of conciliation and compromise; he reflects the dominant psychology of a whole American generation of materialism and reaction which dimmed, along with Douglass and other crisis heroes, the glory and fervor of much early American idealism.

That period, in its turn, is closed or closing. And the principles of Douglass and his times,—the democracy of uncompromising justice and equality, perennially true for all acute observers, emerge from their social and moral eclipse all the more apparent, vital and inescapable. A chronicle of the initial struggles for freedom and social justice is, therefore, particularly pertinent again in our present decade of crisis and social reconstruction. Without undue belittlement, then, of Booker Washington in his time and place of limited vision and circumscribed action, it is only fair and right to measure Douglass, with his militant courage and unequivocal values, against the yardstick, not of a reactionary generation, but of all times. It is thus evident why in the intervening years Douglass has grown in stature and significance, and why he promises to become a paramount hero for Negro youth of today.

This can happen most sanely and effectively if today we read or re-read Douglass's career in his own crisp and graphic words, lest he be minimized or maximized by the biographers. There is most truth and best service in a realistic rather than a romanticized Frederick Douglass. For he was no paragon, without flaw or contradiction, even though, on the whole the consistent champion of human rights and the ardent, ever-loyal advocate of the Negro's cause. His life was full of paradoxes, and on several issues he can be quoted against himself. In the course of events, for example, the man who "unsold himself from slavery" accepted, for expediency at the hands of philanthropic Anti-Slavery friends, the purchase price of his legal freedom; he could whip his overseer and defy, physically and morally, the slaveholder and yet forgive and benefact his old master. He could engage against great odds of personal safety in Anti-Slavery demonstrations in Indiana and elsewhere, and yet counsel John Brown against the Harpers Ferry uprising: in 1850, he declared uncompromisingly for pacifism and peaceful Abolition, but in 1862 pleaded with Lincoln to enlist Negro troops and when the order finally came, sent in his two sons and started out himself as a recruiting agent. More contradictions of this sort could be cited, none more illustrative than the dilemma of intermarriage, which he had to face late in life before the bar of divided public opinion after a long and happy first marriage to his devoted wife, Anna Murray Douglass, a free Negro woman who had befriended him while he was still a slave in Baltimore and who aided him to escape from slavery. Said he to friends, in skillful but incisive self-justification, "In my first marriage I paid a compliment to my mother's race; in my second, to my father's." Whoever reads the full story will doubtless grant him in all cases the tribute of sincerity and courage, and in most instances, too, the vindication of the higher consistency. Douglass's personality, even on its most human side, never lacked the fibre of manhood and manliness.

Douglass's long and close identification with the Anti-Slavery cause, by which he is generally known, obscures his many-sided public life and service. Perhaps his surest claim to greatness came from his ability to generalize the issues of the Negro cause and see them as basic principles of human freedom, everywhere and in every instance. We see him accordingly taking sides with land and labor reforms in England and Ireland when there on a two-year Anti-Slavery campaign. Similarly he became one of the first public advocates of woman's rights and suffrage, attending the first Woman's Rights Convention and becoming the life-long friend and co-worker of Elizabeth Sady Stanton and Susan B. Anthony. His speeches indicate that he clearly saw the land reform objectives of the Free Soil Party, whose first convention he attended in 1852, and was not just attracted by its more obvious bearing in blocking the extension of slave territory. His advocacy of Civil Rights legislation and of free public education similarly showed him far in advance of any narrowly racialist view or stand. It is in this dimension of the progressive publicist and statesman that we need to know in deeper detail of the career of Douglass.

Needing emphasis, too, to do him fuller justice, is his pioneer advocacy of practical vocational education (we find him visiting Harriet Beecher Stowe as early as 1852 with a plan for founding an industrial trade school for Negro youth)—likewise, his early sponsorship of economic organization and business enterprise as a program supplementing educational advancement and political action. All this, when dated, is very impressive as evidence of statesmanship. Indeed, objectives which later seem to have become rivals and incompatibles in the hands of leaders of lesser calibre were, in the conception of Douglass, allies in the common-sense strategy of a common cause. In this respect, he seems, particularly as we read his pithy prose so different from the polished and often florid periods of his orations, a sort of Negro edition of Ben Franklin, reacting to the issues of his time with truly profound and unbiased sanity. It is unusual for a campaigning advocate of causes and a professional orator to be so sane.

Witness his shrewd realistic comment that flanks, in his auto-biography, his impassioned editorial *Men of Color, to Arms!*:—showing him to be by no means the dupe of his own rhetoric,—"When at last the truth began to dawn upon the administration that the Negro might be made useful to loyalty as well as to treason, to the Union as well as to the Confederacy, it then considered in what way it could employ him, which would in the least shock and offend the popular prejudice against him."

Much of his writing has upon it the timeless stamp of the sage. "No people," he says, "to whom liberty is given, can hold it as firmly and wear it as grandly as those who wrench their liberty from the iron hand of the tyrant." . . . "No power beneath the sky can make an ignorant, wasteful, and idle people prosperous, or a licentious people happy." . . . "Neither we, nor any other people, will ever be respected till we respect ourselves, and we will never respect ourselves till we have the means to live respectably." . . . "My hope for the future of my race is further supported by the rapid decline of an emotional, shouting, and thoughtless religion. Scarcely in any direction can there be found a less favorable field for mind or morals than where such a religion prevails." Obviously there is much in Douglass, both of word and deed, which is vital and relevant to this present generation and to our world of today. Racially and nationally we still need the effective re-enforcement of his career and personality. Youth, in its time of stress and testing crisis, needs and can benefit by the inspiring example of a crusading and uncompromising equalitarian.

ROBERT E. HAYDEN [2]

When it is finally ours, this freedom, this liberty, this beautiful
and terrible thing, needful to man as air,
usable as the earth; when it belongs at last to our children,
when it is truly instinct, brain-matter, diastole, systole,
reflex action; when it is finally won; when it is more

[2] From Robert E. Hayden, "Frederick Douglass," *The Atlantic Monthly*, February, 1947, p. 124. Copyright © 1947, by The Atlantic Monthly Company, Boston, Mass. 02116. Reprinted by permission of the publisher.

than the gaudy mumbo-jumbo of politicians:
this man, this Douglass, this former slave, this Negro
beaten to his knees, exiled, visioning a world
where none is lonely, none hunted, alien,
this man, superb in love and logic, this man
shall be remembered—oh, not with statues' rhetoric,
not with legends and poems and wreaths of bronze alone,
but with the lives grown out of his life, the lives
fleshing his dream of the needful, beautiful thing.

Afterword: A Long Shadow

"A sign and a symbol held up for me to see," as H. I. Brock of the New York *Times* wrote of him in 1907,[1] Douglass cast a long shadow. He personified the social mobility characteristics of his countrymen; he embodied the tradition of protest against injustice; and he contributed notably to making American democracy a viable force. Certainly his career is without parallel as a striking example of the American ideal of pulling oneself up by his bootstraps. "Probably no living American has in his personal history experienced such extraordinary vicissitudes of fortune," wrote the *Washington Post* in 1887, upon his return from traveling abroad.[2] Douglass's not inconspicuous achievements take on even greater proportions as they are measured by his obscure origins. From such unheralded beginnings, few Americans went as far.

Greatness was not thrust upon Douglass; he earned it. Believing that success depended upon one's own efforts rather than upon luck, he was a hard worker, the personification of struggle and achievement. He knew what it was to bear the cross of discrimination, but did not believe that prejudice absolved its victims from the exercise of personal responsibility. To obstacles Douglass brought the full resources of a mighty heart. For his success or failure he declined to hold the fates accountable; he did not believe that a man's life is wholly controlled by outside forces. He was fond of quoting Shakespeare's lines, "The fault, dear Brutus, lies not in our stars, but in ourselves, that we are underlings." The New Testament phrase, "He that overcometh," came to life in Douglass.

To democracy in America, Douglass was a whip and spur. He loved his country but he was not blind to its faults. The anomaly of a democracy in which the exercise of freedom was often dangerously circumscribed had led Douglass to assume the role of critic. His life was a protest—a perpetual and burning rebuke against

[1] H. I. Brock, "The Negro," *The South in the Building of the Nation* (Richmond: The Southern Historical Publishing Society, 1909), VII, 530.
[2] *Washington Post* in *Cleveland Gazette*, August 27, 1887.

what he conceived as anti-democratic impulses. Before he reached thirty he had decided that the conscience of America needed an irritant and he stood ready "to blister it all over from the center to circumference." Douglass contributed to American democracy by holding a mirror to it.

Douglass's concept of a good American was broad-gauged; he supported no creed that sought to curtail the rights of others. The championing of the downtrodden in general—this was the reforming task Douglass set for himself. "Now as always," he wrote after he had turned sixty, "I am for any movement whenever and wherever there is a good cause to promote, a right to assert, a chain to be broken, a burden to be removed, or a wrong to be redressed." [3]

As a reformer, Douglass acted as though he believed that nations, like individuals, controlled their destiny. Hence if men worked to make the world better, such would come to pass. Opposition did not dim his hopes; indeed he construed resistance to a cause as a proof of its progress. If reformers—those who cut to the bone social truth and national morality—are necessary antidotes to stagnation in the body politic, Douglass must be accounted among his country's benefactors. More than a protest figure, Douglass affirmed the great ideas upon which his country was founded. Of all the things he ever read, Douglass liked nothing better than the Declaration of Independence. Perhaps without his planning it, he had fashioned his own career on two of the Declaration's great affirmations. During the first half of his public life, he worked for an America in which all men would be endowed with liberty. During the second half of his public life, he worked for an America in which all men would be treated as having been created equal. In fine, Douglass unerringly sensed that the land of his birth was a nation not by a common blood knot, not by a history stretching back into the dim unknown, but by its commitment to the revolutionary concept that all men were created equal.

In the years since his passing, it has become evident that Douglass is no period piece. His life was a kind of documentary of American history when we pause to reflect that the fight against injustice and oppression is a national characteristic whether the date be 1776,

[3] Douglass to C. S. Smith (Bloomington, Illinois), undated, in *Arkansas Mansion*, April 12, 1884.

1895, or today. In this sense the Douglass theme cannot be exhausted. In our own times it has been common for protagonists of this or that program of social action to invoke the Douglass name. Among the present-day titles bestowed upon him is that of "father of the civil rights movement."

During the past decade many "freedom schools" and study groups have named themselves after Douglass. The federal government has followed suit in its fashion. It has purchased his Anacostia Heights home as a national shrine under the National Parks Service of the Department of the Interior; it has named a bridge in the nation's capital after him, and it has issued a twenty-five cent postage stamp of general issue on February 14, 1967, in commemoration of the one hundred and fiftieth anniversary of his birth. Such actions may not be free from political considerations, but whatever their motivation they bespeak an essential truth: that in the career of Frederick Douglass nineteenth century America takes on an added dimension, illuminating those times and reflecting light upon our own.

Bibliographical Note

A prolific writer, Douglass is his own best source of information. He wrote three autobiographies, the first of them, *Narrative of the Life of Frederick Douglass*, published in 1845, selling some 30,000 copies in five years and adding to his fame at home and abroad. Updating this initial autobiography, Douglass, in 1855, published *My Bondage and My Freedom*, a work of 462 pages, well over three times the length of the *Narrative*. His final autobiography, *Life and Times of Frederick Douglass*, came out in 1881. In it Douglass had to foreshorten his slavery and abolitionist experiences in order to include his Civil War and Reconstruction activities. Translations of the first two were made into French, German, and Swedish, and all three autobiographies were reprinted two or more times. Let it be granted that autobiography, in Richard D. Altick's words, is the "product of sober second thought, hindsight and filtered memory." Nevertheless the Douglass autobiographies are remarkably dependable in their factual content—their accuracy as to dates, places, people, and events.

Many of Douglass's editorials, articles, speeches and personal letters are to be found in the periodicals he edited, *The North Star* (Rochester, 1847–51), *Frederick Douglass' Paper* (Rochester, 1851–60), and *Douglass' Monthly* (Rochester, 1859–63). Including many excerpts from these journals, Philip S. Foner has published a massive four-volume work, *The Life and Writings of Frederick Douglass*, an invaluable treasure-house of the important Douglass writings. Foner was a zealous and resourceful collector, but he could not hope to examine the total output of Douglass's writings, some of which are still in private hands, and others of which are scattered in a score or more of manuscript collections and in the columns of fugitive newspapers long defunct.

The Douglass home at Anacostia Heights in Washington, D. C., contains carbon copies of many of Douglass's letters and speeches, plus communications sent to him. These have been placed on microfilm by the Photoduplication Service of the Library of Congress. This was a needed service, although far too little time was given to organizing and arranging the materials before placing them on microfilm.

The book-length biographies of Douglass number a scant dozen. The earlier ones, written shortly before or shortly after his death, were episodic in treatment and uncritical in tone, reeking with hero-worship. The best of this lot is Frederic May Holland, *Frederick Douglas: The Colored Orator* (New York: Funk & Wagnalls Co., Inc., 1891). In writing the book Holland was "badly hurried," as he explained to Douglass in a private letter.[1] Nevertheless he produced a clearly and often dramatically written work which holds the interest despite the frequent insertions of long speeches. Another professional writer who diverted his attention to Douglass was Charles Waddell Chesnutt, the Negro novelist. Small-size and brief, his *Frederick Douglass* (Boston: Small, Maynard and Company, 1899) was essentially an extended essay, with the reader disarmed by Chesnutt's explanation that he had no special qualification as a Douglass life-writer other than "a profound and in some degree a personal sympathy" with his subject.

An even less useful work is James M. Gregory, *Frederick Douglass: the Orator* (Springfield, Mass.: Willey and Company, 1893), which has little to recommend it beyond an introduction by William S. Scarborough and its photographs of the Douglass offspring. John W. Thompson, *An Authentic History of the Douglass Monument* (Rochester: E. Darrow and Company, 1903), is a recital of the efforts to raise money for a Douglass statue in Rochester. Crammed with trivial detail, it does have some interesting inclusions, such as letters from President McKinley, Booker T. Washington, and Elizabeth Cady Stanton; a statement by Susan B. Anthony; a speech by Governor Theodore Roosevelt; an original poem by T. Thomas Fortune; and a eulogy by John C. Dancy. In 1906, Booker T. Washington, then at the zenith of his great career, engaged S. Laing Williams of Chicago to ghostwrite a Douglass biography for him. Written in a direct and easy-to-read style, this Washington-Laing volume (*Frederick Douglass*, Philadelphia, 1906) presented no new facts about the man and never got below the surface. Hence it is of greater interest to Washington scholars than to those seeking light on Douglass.

After this biography there was no book-length study of Douglass for some 40 years, until Benjamin Quarles brought out *Frederick*

---

[1] Holland to Douglass, Aug. 8, 1890. Frederick Douglass Papers, Frederick Douglass Memorial Home. Microfilmed by Library of Congress, Reel 5.

Douglass (Washington: Associated Publishers, Inc., 1948; reprinted New York, 1968). This work "gave a balanced account which portrayed him neither as a demi-god or a demagogue," wrote Rayford W. Logan in the 1962 Collier Books reprint of *Life and Times*. In 1963 Philip S. Foner, consummating earlier plans, brought together the introductions to his four volumes, previously mentioned, and published them under the title, *Frederick Douglass*. A worthy addition to the Douglass literature, this book profited from Foner's extensive researches and professional skills. It is to be noted that Foner is boldly interpretive, often to the point of editorializing.

If one is to measure accurately the importance of Douglass in contemporary history writing, he must go beyond the biographies and take note of the recent significant works which give due attention to him. Thus, for example, in Kenneth Stampp's revisionist history of slavery, *The Peculiar Institution* (New York: Alfred A. Knopf, Inc., 1956), there are more than 20 references to Douglass or his *Narrative*. Louis Filler, in his *The Crusade against Slavery, 1830–1860* (New York: Harper & Row, Publishers, 1960), has fewer references than Stampp, but they are richer in detail. James M. McPherson, *The Struggle for Equality: Abolitionists and the Negro in the Civil War and Reconstruction* (Princeton, N.J.: Princeton University Press, 1964), has 57 references to Douglass, and August Meier, in his highly praised *Negro Thought in America* (Ann Arbor, Michigan: University of Michigan Press, 1963), gives repeated notice to Douglass, viewing him as "the greatest living symbol of the protest tradition during the 1880's and the early 1890's."

Index

A

Abolition, 1, 4–8, 16, 34–43, 59, 61–62, 65, 71, 76–77, 90, 92–97, 99–103, 107–12, 116–18, 138–64, 170–72
  and civil rights, 143–64
  and education, 143
Allen, Willam G., 99, 101
American Anti-Slavery Society, 110, 154
Anthony, Susan B., 172

B

Blaine, James G., 17, 159
Brown, John, 10, 68, 70, 171
Bruce, John Edward, 118–20

C

Calhoun, John C., 62
Civil rights movements, 143–64
Civil War, 1, 7, 10, 11, 76, 78, 138, 139, 143, 146, 154, 171
Clay, Henry, 62, 106
Cleveland, Grover, 17, 159
Confederacy, 11–12, 76, 173
Cook, John E., 68, 69
Covey, Edward, 2, 6, 168

D

Declaration of Independence, 35, 46, 48, 49, 136, 143, 148, 158, 176
Demby, Bill, 25–27
Democratic Party, 17
Douglass, Anna Murray, 3, 15, 171
Douglass, Frederick:
  and abolition, 34, 70, 137, 147–67, 170–73
  as Commissioner of Chicago World's Fair, 121, 123, 126
  as Counsel General to Haiti, 16–17, 119, 125
  criticism of, 15, 107–12, 118–20
  escape from slavery, 28–33, 166, 171
  eulogies to, 122–31

Douglass, Frederick (Cont.)
  ideologies, 146–47, 160–64
  and industrial education, 9, 145, 151, 162, 163, 172
  as orator, 4, 5, 7–17, 38–79, 99–101, 118, 142–44, 154–55
  as U.S. Marshal, 1, 13, 14
  and women's rights movement, 9, 172
Douglass, Helen Pitts, 15, 161
Douglass, Lewis, 4, 141
Douglass, Rosetta, 4
Dred Scott decision, 59, 64, 71, 146
Dubois, W. E. B., 14, 80, 135

E

Emancipation Proclamation, 11, 77, 156
Emigrationists, 151, 154

F

Foner, Phillip S., 138–42
Freedmen, 29, 31, 89, 93, 103, 140, 168
Freeland, William, 2, 3
Free Soil Party 10, 167, 172
Fugitive Slave Law, 65, 146

G

Garfield, James A., 13, 14, 159
Garrison, William Lloyd, 4, 5, 7, 49, 107–12, 128, 135, 167
Gore, Austin, 25–27
Grant, Ulysses S., 72, 128

H

Harpers Ferry, 10, 68–71, 171
Harrison, Benjamin, 16, 159
Hayden, Robert E., 169, 173–74
Hayes, Rutherford B., 1, 13, 90, 159
Higginson, Thomas Wentworth, 99, 101–2

J

Jefferson, Thomas, 48, 75, 139
Job discrimination, 50, 94, 141, 146
Johnson, Andrew, 12, 13